little girl lost...
GROWN
Woman
FOUND

...WALKING OUT OF A DARK PAST INTO A BRIGHT FUTURE.

Allean Danielle

Gloria,
Thank you so
much for the support
& purchase! I pray
you find a blessing
in these pages!
Allean
Danielle

DEDICATION

This book is dedicated to the matchless Lamb of God!
...The innocent One who carried a cross, suffered, bled, died
and rose again on the third day, conquering death, hell and
the grave for little ole' me!...The one who held my hand
through every hardship I've ever endured...The one who
continues to hold my hand daily and never leaves my side.

I am eternally grateful!

FOREWORD

It gives me great pleasure to have this opportunity to say something about this very inspirational book. During my 30 years of pastoring, I have read many books, articles, papers and other materials. *little girl lost...Grown Woman Found* is without question one of the most powerful and inspirational books I have ever read.

This book of poetry gives us permission and tells us it's okay to look back at some of the dark places in our lives that helped shape us into who we are. I believe there is something in this book that will touch the life of every person who is blessed enough to read it. There are stories about pain and perseverance, problems and progress, troubles and triumphs, and many other inspirational messages. In addition, this author asks questions that make you feel compelled to search yourself for the answers needed in your own life.

As I consider this book and the society in which we live, I question how many other lost little girls have not been found. I believe many grown women who are almost found will experience immeasurable blessings by reading this book. This book is not only an inspiration to those who have had similar experiences; it is inspirational as well to anyone who has a healthy appreciation for life, powerful testimony, and feel-good stories. It will reach those who have a deep concern and passion for this society we live in and those who lack the courage to stand up and tell their story.

My brothers and sisters, as a pastor and preacher for so long, I have never read another book that has blessed, helped, and inspired me more than *little girl lost...Grown Woman Found.* I am proud to be pastor and I am even more proud to be the father of this talented and gifted young woman. I am moved to have been asked to foreword this book for a very special writer.

Pastor, John L. Bowen Sr.
Greater Mount Vernon Missionary Baptist Church
Minneapolis, Minnesota

ROAD MAP

Phase 2: *Emotional Roller Coaster*

Phase 3: *Spiritual Cleansing*

Sneak Peak into Volume 2

Acknowledgements

ABOUT THE AUTHOR

Allean Danielle Ward-Thompson is a native of Kankakee, Illinois. She was born on December 9, 1977 to Deneise Ward (Farrow). Dani, as she is known to her family and friends, has one sister (Tangula) and three brothers (Adonis, Maurice & Kurtis). She also has a host of paternal siblings; special recognition to Thearthur, Matthias & Queentanya Scott and Coleman Davis Jr.

Dani values family and enjoys the love and responsibility that comes along with it. She is married to her long time beau, Reverend Shawn Thompson. Together they parent four wonderful children, Lamont, Latrez, BriAija and Destiny.

Dani is a faithful member of Greater Mount Vernon M.B. C. under the leadership of Pastor John L. Bowen Sr. and the mentorship of the lovely Bettye Bowen. She has served in various ministries over the years and currently serves on the Deaconess Board and the Young Adult Ministry, attends and teaches the Women of Destiny (women's ministry) and sings in the Inspirational Choir. Her passion for poetry led her to start Write the Vision youth poetry ministry and Treasures of the Heart adult poetry ministry; she serves as the chairperson for both ministries.

Dani is an honor graduate of North Hennepin Community College having received an Associate's Degree in Liberal Arts in 2009. Immediately following graduation from North Hennepin, she enrolled at Metropolitan State University where she received her Bachelor's of Art Degree in Criminal Justice in 2011. Not one to rest on her laurels, she is preparing to start graduate school to complete her master's degree and has her eyes firmly fixed on pursuing her education in hopes of obtaining a doctorate degree.

Dani has a great love for children and enjoys mentoring and exposing them to positive alternatives. As a mentor to young girls for over a decade, she learned how to rely on her instincts. These instincts, honesty, and a no-nonsense approach have proven to be the recipe to get a breakthrough with the toughest young lady. She also speaks to students, church congregations and community organizations about the abuse she suffered through and how she was able to overcome the pain associated with it. She currently works as an Education Assistant.

Poetry is her outlet and she has been writing ever since she can remember. "Writing is my passion and no matter what I'm doing, in the back of my mind, I'm thinking about something I could or should write."

INTRODUCTION/BACKGROUND

Thank you for purchasing my book of poetry! In this book I invite you to join me as I journey through the items I hold close to my heart. Many of these treasures have been hidden for years and I am excited to share them with you now.

Although I have been writing since I can remember, I have only been sharing my writing for the last eight years. I would like to thank my loving church family for encouraging me to share this gift. Several years ago at our Annual Black History Program, I shared a poem entitled "Which They Are You." It was so well received that I was inspired to share more of my poetry writings, which eventually lead to the book you are holding today. Greater Mount Vernon...I thank you and love you with all my heart! GMV... "We all we got!!"

The poetry you will find in this book contains my journey of abuse and pain inflicted, responses to that abuse and pain, love and love lost, the journey of finding me in the aftermath, my spiritual awakening, reconstruction and rebirth.

Allow me to go back in time and share a few things with you to summarize some of the key points of my journey. My childhood was troubled to say the least. I was in the neighborhood of five years old when I was first sexually molested. This first incident began while my mother was in the hospital giving birth to my youngest brother, and lasted for some time. Even at such a young age, I was very perceptive and I knew what this man was doing to me wasn't right. I also knew this man whom I had called Uncle "so and so," was not my uncle at all. He couldn't have been because none of my Granny's sons had ever done these things to me and I knew in my heart they never would. From the very first time he violated me, I vowed to never call him "uncle" again, and to this day I haven't. I could say a lot more about him, but I'll only say the deepest scars I possess today were inflicted by him. Scars that have hindered me in ways I couldn't begin to describe. Of all the incidents I endured, his was the most grotesque and left me with the most traumas. I was left with emotional and mental trauma that still haunts me to this very day.

A few years ago, I found out he was in jail for molesting his girlfriend's children. After hearing this, I suffered through a period of guilt, regret, and even shame. I felt responsible for what happened to these little girls because I never said anything about what he had done to me. However, I now know even if I had said something, there is no guarantee he wouldn't have had the opportunity to inflict the same torture on them anyway. I also know it was never my guilt, regret, or shame, it was his. I pray for these girls and every girl who has had to endure this horrific experience. My first prayer is that God will give them strength to overcome this huge burden that has been heaped upon them. I also pray for the power and confidence they need to confront their past. And finally I pray for release. Release is a critical factor in becoming a survivor instead of forever remaining a victim. I learned the hard way...Let it go!

Although my childhood didn't start off too bad, over a period of time, our home slowly became the "drinking spot." Sadly, as the drinking in the home increased, the sexual abuse my sister and I suffered through increased as well. It occurred so often, that although I hated every incident, I eventually became numb to it all. As sad as it may seem, it was our way of life. As a small girl, I observed my mama being treated differently by our family members. Once, I heard someone refer to her as the "black sheep" of the family. I assumed it was because of the drinking, but who knows. I heard the others say mean things about my mama, my siblings, and myself. In my finite mind, we simply didn't measure up. I concluded; we weren't accepted because we were an extension of her. I compared myself to my cousins because they were always clean, dressed nicely, had toys, food, electricity, running water and the list goes on. I was just the opposite and I knew it. Several years later, when I was eleven years old, I went to live with my Granny. This is when I began to believe I just might measure up to the rest of the family. This move gave me hope that there was a different way of life and I considered myself "normal".

If my home life didn't succeed in robbing me of my confidence and self-worth, life at school surely would. I was a total outcast among my peers. My weakness and unwillingness to stand up for myself aided them in becoming professionals at singling me out, taunting, teasing, and berating me on a daily basis. At first, it wasn't because I was mean or had a bad attitude. It was simply because of what I didn't have. It was because I didn't wear new clothes and new shoes and because the clothes and shoes I wore were never clean. It was because my clothes and shoes were old, raggedy, and because I smelled.

I recall an incident I am sure I'll never forget. I had to be in the 2nd or 3rd grade. I was standing in a circle of about six girls. One girl said, "I have a secret." She then whispered into the ear of the girl next to her and they both smiled. The girl who had been told the secret then whispered it to the girl next to her. They all took their turns whispering, smiling, some laughing out loud and all of them looking directly at me. When the girl next to me was told the secret, I heard what was said..."Allean stinks like pee." It floored me as they all continued to laugh. My mouth and nostrils closed, refusing air and I felt as if my heart had stopped beating. I was too embarrassed to move and too scared to cry because I thought crying would make it worse. I simply tried to act as if I didn't hear. In almost a whisper I said, "Tell me." At this point they all looked at me, started laughing more intensely, and walked away. I hated those girls. I hated them for being mean and for not having a heart. I hated them for not caring enough to find out why I smelled like pee. I hated them for having "perfect parents." Their perfect parents bought them nice clothes, combed their hair, and provided for them so they didn't have to come to school dirty and smelly. Of course, I later found out no one has perfect parents. Some children are simply blessed to have parents who provide f or them. Children whose parents choose not to or are not able to provide for their children, for whatever reason, are valued no less than those who do. As much as I hated these girls, I hated my situation even more. I did smell and there was nothing I could do about it. I had horrible nightmares because of the abuse I was suffering through and I wet the bed just about every night. At the time, we didn't have running water at home. I was forced to go to school and the fact that I smelled like urine didn't make a bit of difference.

Being an outcast at school, coupled with the issues at home, fueled a fire within me. I found myself caught up in a terrible whirlwind of anger. Now my peers had a reason not to like me. I was mean and angry and would lash out in an instant. Needless to say, I fought a lot in school. Once again the reasoning of my finite mind convinced me everyone else was exempt from the pain I experienced on a daily basis. I was the only one suffering. Therefore, I gave myself the responsibility of inflicting the pain that was being inflicted upon me onto others. Fighting was the solution to every negative situation I faced. I now know what an erroneous concept that was.

In addition to the anger, I also became very promiscuous. Though I've never tried recreational drugs, I can be honest enough to admit, men were my drug of choice. As vulgar as this will sound, I clung to sex...I needed it. I was exposed to it at an early age and it was always there. In a sense, I needed it because it was all I had ever known. I was "over-sexed". Another explanation for my promiscuity lies within a deep-rooted desire to be loved. However, my attempts to fill this desire failed miserably because I equated sex with love. I was oblivious to the fact that sex didn't have anything to do with true love. Because I thought sex and love were interchangeable, I made a lot of bad decisions. I freely gave myself to boys/men who didn't even deserve to know my name. I pushed some great men away because of my approach. I also held on to some men I shouldn't have given the time of day. As I look back on some of the situations and relationships in which I have been involved in, I can't do anything short of shake my head in disbelief. At times I feel as if I simply wasted too much of my life on the wrong men. All of it ended in abuse and pain!

My desire to be loved resulted in a bad miscarriage at the age of fourteen. This loss of love sparked another desire within in me; the desire to have someone of my own to love. Less than a year later, I was intentionally pregnant with my first son, Lamont. At age sixteen, I moved in with my boyfriend, and dropped out of high school. And at age eighteen, I gave birth to my second son, Latrez. Soon after the birth of my second son, I returned to school and received my G.E.D. Upon completion of my G.E.D., my quest for higher education was kindled and I enrolled in Kankakee Community College. I then broke ties with the father of my boys and began the journey of "single motherhood." After three brief semesters in community college, this single mother of two had to drop out to obtain a second job to support my family. At the age of twenty-three, I gave birth to my third child, BriAija.

It was at this point that I truly started to evaluate my life. I was sick and tired of working dead-end jobs, being in dead-end relationships, and especially tired of what my surroundings had to offer me and my children. Close examination of my family's lifestyle and that of people who looked like me in the area, left me with little hope of my children finding success in Kankakee. I don't want to give the impression that it's impossible to remain in Kankakee, beat the odds and find success because that's not true. I'm simply saying I didn't know how to remain in that environment and prepare my children for success.

We lived in an apartment complex in which shootings were an everyday occurrence. At one point my then seven-year-old son had grown so accustomed to the shootings they neither bothered nor scared him. Although my children had their own bedrooms and beds, I was so afraid for their safety, I made a pallet on the floor of my bedroom for them to sleep. I can recall an incident in which we were lying down for the night and I thought I heard guns shots. I asked my son if he heard it. Just as casual and unemotional as he could, his reply was, "I don't know, Mom. Good night." He pulled the covers up to his neck, closed his eyes, and went to sleep. I lay there in shock staring at him, trying to wrap my brain around the idea of a seven-year-old who was no longer frightened by the sound of gunshots. I was trying to envision how a seven-year old could peacefully lie down and go to sleep while shots were being fired around him. The reality of my situation generated a yearning and a drive within me to get out of Kankakee, Illinois.

However, Kankakee was all I knew. My entire family was there, so moving was one of the hardest things I've ever had to do in my life. In the end, I simply weighed the odds with questioning; a method that seldom fails me! What do I want for my children? What could I possibly offer them here? How can I better equip them with the tools necessary for success? Would a new environment offer them more opportunities and better chances to succeed? Would a fresh start provide an opportunity for me to recreate our lives? I watched various family members both young and old take their place in the revolving door of penal institutions almost as if it was their destiny or birthright. Is this what being a "Ward" was all about? Is this what being a black male in Kankakee was all about? Because if it was, I wanted no parts of it! Although it wasn't set in stone that my children would choose this road, there was a high likelihood they would. So, I visited several places to see what they had to offer. One year later, I packed up my family and relocated to Minnesota where I currently reside.

Shortly after moving to Minnesota, I met Shawn Thompson. What I didn't know at that time was this man would steal my heart and eventually make me his wife. Although we bonded right away, our young love would be tested many times before we got it right. After two years of dating, Shawn moved back to Kankakee and it seemed we were done for good. Before this happened, we had conversations about getting into church but had never taken the initiative to do so. Once Shawn left, I spoke to my Auntie Von about her church and the devil got busy! Every time I attempted to go to church, something happened to prevent it. One Sunday I even got into a car accident! By the grace of God, I finally walked through the doors of Greater Mount Vernon M.B.C., and my life changed forever! It was inside the walls of this church that I surrendered to God and allowed Him to begin a mighty work in my life.

Before I gave my life to Christ, I didn't believe I could be healed from the scars of my past. Now I thank God for His miraculous healing powers. He lovingly accepted me into His bosom. In doing so, He filled the void I couldn't fill myself with the fighting, men, or any other thing else I had previously tried to use. God gave me an extraordinary under-shepherd who not only taught me the Word but how to study it for myself. In addition to his phenomenal preaching and teaching, this shepherd also counseled me through the issues of my past and adopted me as his daughter.

Shawn returned to Minnesota a year later and became a member of GMV. He then accepted his calling to preach and we were married shortly thereafter. Our family became complete when my niece Destiny moved to Minnesota and became our daughter. God has surrounded me with genuine, kind-hearted, loving people who embraced me and my family as if we were of blood relation. I owe my transformation to God and this wonderful support system. This new "me" was the last piece of the "finding myself" puzzle. Now a complete person, I am able let go and let God!

So after years of physical and sexual abuse, ridicule and shame at the hands of my peers for being less fortunate, using my fists to solve my problems, confusing sex with love, dropping out of school at sixteen years old, becoming a teenage mother with two children by age eighteen, failed relationship after failed relationship, after years of feeling lonely and unworthy of love...Wandering aimlessly through life without any direction or purpose. Finally, I went back to school to get my G.E.D., worked hard and earned two college degrees, finally I know the difference between love and sex, finally I am content and know my worth, finally I am intelligent enough to advocate with words and I don't have to resort to violence to solve my problems, finally I can be a positive influence for my children, I finally found true love, finally I found the truth and surrendered my life to Jesus Christ, finally this ugly duckling has transformed into a beautiful swan...

Finally this little girl lost
...Is now a Grown Woman Found!

Enjoy!

little girl lost...
GROWN
Woman
FOUND

...WALKING OUT OF A DARK PAST INTO A BRIGHT FUTURE.

Allean Danielle

Mic Check

Mic Check 1...2
Testing 1...2...3
...Is This Thing On? (Clears Throat)

I have these grandiose ideas of fame
For my name to be surrounded by lights
The thought of my picture on billboards
Makes me squeal in sheer delight
I exaggerate my fantasies
Because pure unadulterated motivation is rare
I exude hope and encouragement into every word
So my readers know I care

I have a slight inclination on becoming a best seller
And people tell me it will be an easy feat
So I write to my heart's content
And pass out cards to everyone I meet
I study words diligently
And daily I add to the dictionary in my head
I write as if it's going out of style
And continuously pray to be Spirit led
I am inclined to intense interrogation
Of each word as I prepare a phrase
I think about how my words will touch my readers
Defeat is not an option...
So with each poem my standards I raise

From negative to positive
Is the journey in which I embark
To change my speech patterns to light from dark

No more expletives...I now speak life

I now encourage others
Since I've let go of the strife
I now realize true intelligence
Is displayed in verbal communication
I don't need verbal fillers to falsify dedication

My passion for writing is my drive
And helping someone else is my motivation
But I won't set my sights to high
In order to avoid devastation
I place this book in the Lord's hands
And pray...His Will be done
And if I never become a best seller
At least I'll have had loads of fun
As if I'd sold a million books
I'll remain just as content
Why not be elated?
My name and legacy are in print!
For future generations to read
And to apply my words if need be
To encourage them to face difficulty
With love and forgiveness...Not begrudgingly

Mic Check 1...2 (Irritated Sigh)
Testing 1...2...3 (Annoyed Exhale)
...Is This Thing On? (Smacks Lips)
(Shrugs Shoulders...Drops Mic...Walks Off Stage)

Bio/I Am Poem

Allean Danielle
Strong, gorgeous, courageous, loving and kind
Daughter of Deneise
Sibling of Tangula, Adonis, Maurice and Kurtis
Mother of Lamont, Latrez, BriAija & Destiny
Lover of peace, respect, kindness and charity
Who fears no one but God
Who needs affection and attention
Who gives guidance, encouragement & direction
Who would like to see us all get along
Resident of
The village who raises children together
Ward-Thompson
I am loving and kind
I wonder why people kill each other
I hear children crying
I see life as it should be
I want racial & judicial harmony
I am loving and kind
I pretend to have it all together
I feel like a sheep ready for the slaughter
I touch the hearts of many
I worry about abused children
I cry when children are abused
I am loving and kind
I understand the world is unfair
I say we should all take a stand
I dream of equality for everyone
I try to treat everyone with kindness
I hope one day we'll all get it together
I am loving and kind

Vernacular of Love

As I whisper these poetic phrases into the atmosphere
The cataclysmic upheaval of melodious rhythms
enter the stratosphere
My harmonious declaration

breaks the sound barrier with lightning speed

Mind, body and soul are united
as I receive the strength to proceed
Words roll off my tongue with ease
as I appease ears and quiet fears
My uncanny ability to turn a phrase
will reduce a grown man to tears
I hear your guards coming down

as I arouse your inner being with these sounds

I use my vernacular of love to capture you in my rapture
After I have you hooked
I carry you off to lovely lands of solitude and ecstasy
And give you an overdose of expression
that will jostle your brain

Though the change is strange and you adapt in pain
Enchanted by my words you will forever remain
Mesmerized
     by
         my
              spectacular
                        vernacular
                                  of
                                        love...

A Place Where...

I come from a place where...
They spit on the broom if you sweep their feet
So they didn't go to jail

A place where...
If you ain't make it home before the streetlights came on
They beat yo tail

A place where...
The milk didn't come out of a jug
But out of a box because it was powder

A place where...
If you helped mama make macaroni for dinner
It *literally* took an hour
(Thick government cheese...LBVS)

A place where...
We washed clothes in the back yard
Trying not to get our hands & arms stuck in the wringer

A place where...
You knew when you were close to the dam
Because the smell had a tendency to linger

A place where…
We made jewelry out of lightning bugs
And enjoyed the sound of locusts
When the sky began to lose its light

A place where…
The rats and roaches acted like they paid rent
And if a cricket got in the house
You were up all night

A place where…
We didn't have much at all
In the way of financial possessions
And it seemed like fantasies were the only hope we had

A place where...
Back then it seemed
We were at the bottom of the totem pole
But we now realize it really wasn't all that bad

A place where…
I sometimes long to be
Those times when I'm missing the good ole' days
…In Kankakee

I Couldn't Love You More

Your blood doesn't flow through my veins
But you're my dad just the same
You took a sad, confused little girl
Equipped her with knowledge that changed her game
I couldn't love you more
…If I were born with your last name
I used to say you can't miss what you never had
I never knew how much I needed one
…Until you became my dad
You took me into your arms
And showed me love in every way
You're responsible for the submission
That allowed the Lord to mold me
Into the woman I am today
I couldn't love you more
… If you were there from the very first day
You taught me, I'm not my past
That what happened to me was out of my control
Told me that in order for me to have a future
I had to break free from anger's hold
You helped me draw up a new blueprint
Helped me strategically place the pieces on my chest board
I couldn't love you more
…If you cut my umbilical cord
When I thought generational curses
Would block any possibility of a blessing
You spoke life into my troubled existence
Through numerous counseling sessions

You assured me God loves me
And that He will help me
Pick up the pieces of my brokenness
Encouraged me to depend on the Lord more
And to worry less
I couldn't love you more
…If the breath in my body came from your chest

Over the years we've shared
Smiles, frowns, loads of fun
Buckets of tears and barrels of laughs
Countless teaching moments to get me on the right path
Progress and setbacks; anger and sorrow
Irreplaceable memories I'll cherish every tomorrow
If you held my tiny hands
And guided me as I took my first steps
If you taught me how to ride a bike
If you hugged me on the first day of school
And assured me everything would be alright
If you scolded and punished me
The first time I stayed out late all night
If your iris pigmentation determined my eye color
And established the ability of my seeing
If your DNA was the molecule
That encoded the genetic instructions
Responsible for developing me into a living being
I could not possibly love you more than I do today
Some say I'm lucky…I say I'm blessed
I thank God for you daily
…You're simply the best

Thanks for everything Dad!!

PHASE 1

Abuse & Pain

The Heart Feels What the Eyes Can't See

"Scars are a sign of survival; they don't bleed and are not sensitive to the touch. We need to stop hemorrhaging and thank God we're alive!"
—Reverend John L. Bowen Sr.

The content in this phase is deep and somewhat dark. I have experienced and survived a lot of pain and what I consider suffering in my short life. I would be the first to admit that I do not have a monopoly on pain and suffering. I know there are many people in this world who have suffered in ways I couldn't begin to imagine. However, my pain was and is real to me and writing has helped me heal my wounds. It is mainly during these "dark" times that I have used writing as an outlet. I write to soothe my pain. I write because I know healing follows a positive outlet. Most importantly, I write to keep myself in check.

At times my writing includes ranting and raving that could be misconstrued as that of an "angry black female." That couldn't be further from the truth. I simply write more when I am in difficult situations. However, I have been blessed enough to realize the situations I've been through were temporary. I have always known I have the power to choose what's best for me in my life. I could allow painful situations to become stumbling blocks or I could use them as stepping stones. The pain of my past was once a massive stumbling block that held me in bondage for a long time. In many ways I hated myself for what I had been through. I learned the hard way, self-hate is the worst hate and now I'm done with that phase of my life. I now choose to use any situation that is not indicative of forward progress as a stepping stone. Although my past has played an integral part in shaping and molding me, it does not dictate nor does it define who I am. I have made some mistakes, such as becoming angry, teen-aged pregnancies, dropping out of school, confusing sex with love and the list goes on. However, continuous self-evaluation has aided me in redirecting my anger and seeing my worth.

In my personal experience, painful things were often swept under the rug. And to that I say, never leave painful things as they are. I believe we have to learn to confront our past if we expect to have a different type of future. Often times after "the cover-up," we fear digging up our past because of the pain associated with it or how it might make others feel. However, there is healing in these experiences and we can avoid a lot of bad decisions and wrecked relationships in our future if we deal with our past. Whether we choose to admit it or not, pain, bitterness and resentment tends to linger for years because we feel like some people could have done a better job in certain situations. I think it is important to talk through your pain. If necessary we should involve others who played a major role...Not to blame but to heal. I'm not saying it's easy to talk through difficult situations. In fact, having done it myself, I know it is very difficult. In spite of the difficulty, it has helped me tremendously.

I began this compilation of poetry near the end of 2011. Early on, I knew a conversation would need to occur between me and my mother. Over the years, I intentionally delayed this conversation just as I had since I was a small child. When I was eleven years old, an incident occurred in which my sister brought forth allegations of abuse. Due to extenuating circumstances, no one believed her and she was branded a promiscuous liar by our family. Though I never saw her being abused by this person, I know she was telling the truth. I also know my cousin was telling the truth when she came forward and another cousin before her. The fear of not being believed and shame (unnecessary shame) led me to put my experiences in a vault where they have remained for all these years. Over the past five to six years, I have been sharing these experiences with those in need of encouragement. In 2012, I taught a lesson about the heartbreaking story of Tamar (David's daughter). I presented this lesson entitled *A Desolate Woman* to our women's ministry (Women of Destiny). As I taught this lesson on both Tamar and myself, an exchange occurred. Other women began to open up and share their individual experiences involving abuse. Healing took place as we all shared, cried, and even laughed together. When I left the church, I immediately called my mama. We had a long overdue discussion about the things I had placed in the vault. She allowed me to unload with almost no interruption and she accepted everything I had to say. I now realize I held on to all that pain, hurt, and shame when I didn't have to...

Too Many He's to Name

HE took my innocence when I was five
And my life would never be the same
I can still see his face & of course I remember his name
His scent still burns my nose
The stench so raunchy and stale
He was my cousin's dad
The first reason I grew up hating males
He put it in my mouth and hit me when I refused
He left me feeling hurt, angry, sad, and confused

HE was my step-dad's nephew
He moved in fresh out of jail
At eight years old on a pallet on Chestnut Street
Is where his violation of my body unveiled
He grabbed me roughly and told me he loved me
Left scars and bruises where no one could see
Nearly 30 years later these scenes still play in my mind
Not one scene is pleasant…Not gentle…Not kind

HE got me during the summer at my aunt's house
Repeatedly during the night
I couldn't understand why & I knew it wasn't right
We were blood relatives
And this went on for quite some time
This one bothered me the most
Because his face looked like mine

Our paths crossed recently
God knows I didn't want them to

But please believe he now realizes

The hell he put me through
He shared with me heartfelt shame
Remorse and regret
Of course I forgive him but hard as I try
I can't forget

HE was my cousins' brother and he was the very last one
Who would touch me against my will
After this one I was done
I was 13 years old and I flirted with him daily
I told people he was my boyfriend
And I wanted to have his baby
One night I was asleep on the couch
And when I woke up he was inside me
At this point I was so confused about sex
I bragged about it proudly
My cousin brought me back to reality
When she told me I'd been raped
I thank her with all my heart
For giving me the guidance to escape
This nightmare of ignorance
Involving a 21-year-old man
There will never be another *HE*

...*I* boldly took a stand

Premeditated Theft of Childhood

He preys on the innocent...He relies on their trust
To unleash his sick perversion
His nastiness, his wicked lust
He devises a plan to get close
And plays his part real good
His sick and twisted game
...Premeditated theft of childhood

I know he's on his way before he comes
As soon as everyone is asleep he surely does
He's cold, cunning, calculated and callous
This vulture opens the door and enters the room
He creeps in with well thought out malice
He has evil intentions that will be carried out
He's banking on the fact that this little girl won't shout
Because trust and authority have been gained
Threats are rarely needed
And by twisting these two circumstances
Is how these perverts have succeeded

I lie there trying to fake sleep
With my eyes half way open
Praying for a miracle
Quiet as a mouse...Hoping
Somebody, anybody please!
I don't wanna do this stuff
At the same time praying I can go along with it
Because if I don't...He'll get rough

If fear hadn't closed my throat
I would scream as loud as I could
He's positive I won't
...Premeditated theft of childhood

Auntie's new boyfriend
Always tells me how pretty I am
He sets me on his lap
And when I get up I can hardly stand
He gives me money after we collect empty cans
And comes into my bedroom most nights
He says it's time to have some fun
I lie there in deep agony...Far from delight
I just want him to be done and for him to stop doing these things
I wanna talk to mama, but I don't think she'll believe me

He didn't mistakenly cross paths with your child
No, he is the one who was invited in
He's not a stranger at all
He's their new stepdad, uncle
Or simply the family friend
He didn't watch her walking to the bus stop
Or stalk her from his car
He lives with her in her own home
That's where most perverts are
Banking on your trust...Relying on your ignorance
Gaining your acceptance is also used in his defense
I love your child...I could never do what she said I did
Who are you going to believe...Me or this kid?

He preys on the innocence
He relies on their trust
To unleash his sick perversion
His nastiness, his wicked lust
He devises a plan to get close
And plays his part real good
His sick and twisted game
...Premeditated theft of childhood

Bet Not Tell Nobody but God

He told me I bet not tell nobody but God
Cause it would kill my mama
I'm trying not to take it literally
But somehow I know I oughta
Its excruciating pain
It takes everything within me not to holla
So I follow my heart & reach out to my higher power
Our Father which art in Heaven
Hallowed would be thy name
Lord please give me the strength
To deal with this pain
Give me guidance and direction on how to maintain
I'm confused Lord
And sick and tired of being used and abused
I can't continue to live by his rules
I choose to let my mama know
But the trick is to get out of here alive
I'm hoping my intentions don't show
I know, I know
I can do all things through you
Because in you is where my strength lies
For now I'll just lay here
I can't stand the sight of his face
…So I'll just close my eyes

Little Girl

There once was a little girl
And as early as the tender age of two
There was no one there to protect her
And there was nothing she could do
For many days and in many ways
Men violated her body & soul
They took away her innocence
Over the years she became rigid and cold
With no one to turn to
All she could do was hold this in
But this was the worst mistake she made
This mistake sent her to the pen

One bright and sunny day
At the age of 13
A large man approached her roughly
His intent was easily seen
The girl was scared
But more than that she was angry
And she was determined not to let him succeed
So she pulled out her knife and stabbed him twice
Because she refused to meet his sick need
Two weeks later in a padded room in an asylum
She was very shocked to discover
She had killed someone
Stabbing them over one hundred times
And that it wasn't a stranger at all
…It was her mother

This poem is fictitious

The Death of Innocence

The mind of the abused

Is sick, twisted and brilliant all at the same time

Demented memories and dreams of abuse, rape & incest

That has taken place between these thighs

The screams are in my head

Terror and shame won't let them out

So my nights are full of silent cries

At first there was a false sense of neediness

Therefore a premature sexual appetite began to rise

A journey of boys and men were then used by the abused

To fulfill her sexual highs

I was let down, left alone and unprotected

Yet I felt an inner peace

And I knew I had the strength to try

So I let my past be the past and time heal my wounds

What were once wet tears…Are now dry

Although I have forgiven these men and let go of the hate

A question for my abusers managed to survive

Can you look into my eyes and tell me why

At such an early age

…My innocence had to die?

Angry Girl

Slap slap kick punch slap

Inwardly confused
Because I was abused
Not sure how to portray this hurt
So violence I choose

Kick kick punch slap kick

Don't look in my direction
This ain't what you want
I seek out a fight
It's what feels right
If I can get just enough pressure on your neck
I bet I could turn off your lights

Punch punch slap kick punch

This rage inside me desperately needs an escape
I could learn to channel this anger
But I have no patience to wait
I don't want anyone in my business
So get out of my face

Slap slap kick punch slap

I don't want to talk anyone about my issues
I'm too ashamed to admit any of it
If one more person brings this up
I'll have another fit

Kick kick punch slap kick

The Little Girl's Eyes

It's scary what is often seen through the eyes of a child
How harsh things seem to them
When to adults the same things seem so mild

One little girl
Saw things totally different than those around her
Things that others thought irrelevant
Caused her mind to stir

When looking at the world…
The little girl's eyes saw it
As impatient and unkind
Because it housed many people
Who let her down like clockwork
…Time after time

When looking at her peers…
The little girl's eyes saw ridicule & meanness
They never gave her a chance
They just judged her based on her appearance

When looking at her abusers…
The little girl's eyes saw nasty, disgusting, smelly men
Some tried to pass themselves off as "uncles"
Others simply called themselves "family friends"

When looking at her family...
The little girl's eyes saw hypocritical adults

Guiding terrified kids
In some instances they provided protection
In other cases they let the abusers in

When looking at her mother...
The little girl's eyes saw
Sadness, confusion, frustration & sorrow
Her grief caused her to numb herself
In order to get through each day
And she had no hope at all for tomorrow

When looking in the mirror...
The little girl's eyes saw ugliness, shame & self-hate

She didn't see anything remotely close
To whom she actually was
"Who am I to love myself, no one else does?"

All of us can change the view
...Seen through the eyes of a child!

From the Inside Out

There once was a sweet, kind and lovable little girl
But fear, hurt, anger and pain wouldn't let these through
She was talked about & picked on
By her peers all day at school
And at home during the night
She was raped, molested and abused

She was once a happy-go-lucky type of kid
One who was embraced by the world
But when these things were inflicted upon her
Everything changed for this little girl
From the head of the class
To the one after the last
From smiles to frowns
Too few ups and too many downs

From the inside out she was self-destructing
If something didn't change soon
…She'd surely go insane
From the inside out she was losing strength
Slowly she was being overpowered by the pain

Daily she carried this burdensome load
She held so much in she thought she would explode
She felt she had no release
Of course someone would've listened
But she couldn't bring herself to speak
Of these terrible things that were happening to her
The mere thought of these things
Sent her mind in a blur

It hurt too much to think about it
She couldn't imagine telling someone
Her mind became a torturous chamber
And soon she would become undone
She couldn't focus on anything
And felt like her life had no purpose
From the inside out she was mentally killing herself
Trying to figure out what she'd done to deserve this

Mentally, physically and emotionally
She was on overload
Desperately trying to contain this monstrous burden
All on her own she battled this demon
She just couldn't seem to win
Until one day she broke her silence
…And peace poured in

Generational Curse or Learned Behavior?

Words that should never be uttered...Exclaimed!
Words that should be exclaimed...Never uttered?
The daily goings on in a family
Led by angry fathers & mothers
Anger and violence the order of the day
Quick to curse out or smack a kid
Because they're in the way
Generational curse or learned behavior?

Hate spewed daily
No one ever says I love you
Kids growing up sad and confused
No guidance on what they should do
Generational curse or learned behavior?

Adults having more sex with kids
Than they do with their spouse
So many secrets
They could fill a house
Money spent on alcohol, crack, heroin, speed & weed
Everyone's either drunk or high
No one cares enough to meet the children's needs
Generational curse or learned behavior?

Kids being
Verbally, physically, sexually & mentally traumatized
No hugs, no kisses, no one looks into their eyes
No choice left and no way to carry this heavy load
Many run away, some self-destruct, others implode
Then some unknowingly teach this behavior to their kids
They simply do what their "parents" did
Generational curse or learned behavior?

But there are also some
Who buck against this dysfunctional system
They make a conscious choice to live differently
…By writing their own destiny
They don't drink or use drugs
They love, they cherish
They break the silence and confront the past
The only thing they assault is dysfunction & complacency
When this is the case…Contentment won't last
Generational curse or learned behavior?

Generational curses and learned behavior
Go by two different names
But look a little closer and you'll discover
…They're one in the same
Generational curses only exist because a certain behavior is taught
Learned behavior turns into generational curses
Because we accepted when we should've fought

Teach and reinforce positive learned behavior
And break the generational curse!

Seeing Is Believing

Seeing is believing

And so far I have not seen

Of all the trials and tribulations I've been through

I've only figured out what a few mean

I won't say I don't believe

For that is not entirely true

What I am saying is

I just need a bit of proof

This proof can only come from you

Through all the bad times

The only one I saw on my side was me

My mind wanders back to the footprints

I'm trying to uncover the mystery

If you could give me a sign

Just a little something saying you're there

I would give all my love and gratitude

For letting me know you care

I have come a long way

But of course I have a long way to go

If you could show you had a part in this

My appreciation to you I'd owe

A Desolate Place

Thick

rich sands

Dusty

dry wasteland

Thorns and thistles scattered

Torn and tattered

Soul

feels shattered

Lost sight of everything

that once mattered

Bruised and battered

Spit on and abused

Cursed out and misused

Broken hearted and discontent

Short lit

fuse

Sorting through

mistruths

Myself?

...I'm sure to lose

Feelings

Feelings of anger, sorrow and depression
Not yet able to find an outlet for all this aggression
Thinking of many ways I could end it all
But not entirely sure I'm ready to make that call
Sitting here numb to everything around me
I've been through almost everything possible
Why would this be?
If there is a man upstairs why did he choose this for me?
I couldn't have gone wrong
This consists of my memory
How can a child at such a young and tender age

Be to blame for all this turmoil, abuse and rage
Hatred, pain, anger and scars that will last my lifetime
I have to keep it away from my children
This won't happen to mine
If I could turn back the hands of time

I surely would
But since I can't
This line of thought does no good
Please give me a sign of what to do
Someone has an answer
...Is it you?

Pain

Pain?
Oh yeah I've had hurt and pain
There were times I couldn't even see through the rain
That was the tears I cried from my eyes
Due to the pain deep down inside that I tried to hide
My pain didn't turn me into a monster
My pain didn't result in me needing a sponsor
However, my pain
Did make me want to do some things I shouldn't
Do some things some of you probably wouldn't
I tried to stop plenty times…But couldn't
I talked to family and friends
About these men
I prayed the cycle would end
But the more I prayed
The more I would depend and spend
Too much energy and time trying to make him mine
Trying to stop him
From chasing this dime and that dime
To turn him into
The man his father never taught him to be
To get him to see the committed and dedicated me
But just as life sometimes goes
He chose & he chose & he chose
To take that destructive road
The life full of sorrow
Here today, gone tomorrow
But I suppose…As a matter of fact I know for a fact
Once I stop going back
My pain will come to the end of its track

Queen of the Streets

She's now queen of the streets
But she wasn't always
Thinking of her now makes me remember
Back to her younger days
I thought she was beautiful
Light-skinned, long hair and soft brown eyes
But everyone else couldn't see it
They always made her cry
Why are people so mean and cruel?
Is what I would ask
But she let them get her down
I just let it pass
She was never really strong willed
And was always very easily led
I know that's why she ended up in so many men's beds
I couldn't wait for her to teach me things
Not really sure of what they were
Ironically, instead of her teaching me
I ended up teaching her
Since the age of 13 she's been in these streets
And I don't see her coming home soon
Trickin', trampin', druggin' and drinkin'
She's bound to meet her doom
If there is a Lord in Heaven above
Please help her find her way
She's suffered so much for what was inflicted upon her
Is there a bigger price to pay?
Exiled from her family is where she wants to be
I try not to worry about her because I know
…She's finally free!

Help Me Save Her

She's still wet behind the ears
But she thinks she holds the keys to the mysteries of life
In the palm of her hand
She's very confused about love and what it is
So she gets her validation from a man

Common sense doesn't exist
So healthy relationships are hit and miss

Yet and still she insists she has it all together
Whether she realizes it or not
She's in a downward spiral
Her ignorance is viral and contagious to say the least
And this beast within her has taken front and center
It's frozen her heart and now true love can't enter

She clings to those who mean her no good
She disrespects & neglects
To show love to those she should
She's destroying her life and ruining her health
Somebody please help me save her from herself

She's on the fast track to self-destruction
And she doesn't have a clue
Although I love her my love has no bearing
That's why I make this appeal to you…

Somebody...Please!
…Help me save her from herself!

Seasons Change

As the seasons change
So do our lives rearrange
As the leaves fall and cover the ground
So does loneliness start to hang around
As fall abruptly changes to winter
So does an old love from my past re-enter
As the snow falls & becomes one with the earth
So do we bond and our relationship finds worth
As the bitter cold and wind becomes all too real
So does that old flame spark inside for me to feel

However...

As I sit and watch the sun rest
So do his secrets begin to manifest
As the sun begins to set while the earth spins
So do I try to understand this web of deceit I'm in

As the moon is destined to the sky
So do I think I was destined to figure out his lies
Just as the warn summer nights turn briskly cold
So do the feelings I have for him in my soul
As summer, spring, fall and winter will always be
So do I now know, love will always be a mystery

Seasons Change!

We'll Meet Him Again

When my mama first told me he left us
I didn't even cry
I couldn't make myself believe he was gone
Because I didn't want to is why
I tried to be strong I tried to hold in my tears
But the emotions soon overwhelmed me
Out came my worst fears
He had really gone to Heaven
He just up and left us all
I didn't even get a chance to say good-bye
…This is where the tears would fall

The more tears I dropped
The better I began to feel
The more tears I dropped
The more my heart healed
I thought back to the fun times with him
In which I was fortunate enough to share
I remembered how caring & attentive he was
And how when I needed him, he was always there
To know Pah-Pah was to love him
I'm sure all who knew him would agree
I try not to think about how much I miss him
Instead I remember how much he taught me
So try not to let it consume you
Be patient if you can
Just hold on to the fact
We'll all meet him again

In Loving Memory of my grandfather

Cornell "Pah-Pah" Ward Sr.

Far Too Precious for This World

On May 22, 2013
God sent a special delivery to earth
A tiny little baby boy announced his birth
At 1 pound 4 ounces his life would begin
Melvin Marcell Keys Jr.'s fragile body
Housed the strength of ten men
No one knew what joy his short journey would entail
God sent with him special instructions
For Destiny & Marcell
He said:
I give you this gift both precious and rare
With him you must promise to use
Special tender love & care
He will light up your world
Give you meaning for your existence
He will teach you true love, dedication and persistence
Treat each day like it's your last
Don't take one day for granted
The short time I've given you is confusing
But you don't have to understand it
Just know
...He's far too precious for this world
They took heed to God's instructions
And visited him every day
Were deeply involved his precious journey
Showed him love in every way
They surrounded him with a strong support system
Of family & friends to carry out this task
We all took part and celebrated his milestones
And made loving memories that will last

On July 15, 2013
God spoke again He said:
Thank you for taking care of my child
For learning what I sent him to teach
For embracing him with love and kindness
And in his times of need
For always being within reach

Just like you, I have seen his suffering
Just like you, I have seen his pain
Though I also see what you could never see
And human words could never explain
After 54 days he has shown you
You're capable of loving
Beyond your wildest imagination
That you could put someone else's best interests
Before your own without hesitation
I need you to hold him tightly and get your last kisses
I need you to say your last good-byes
I understand your sorrow I understand your cries
But I must take him now and I need you to let him go
In your heart of hearts you have to know

...He's far too precious for this world!

In Loving Memory of my first grandchild
Melvin Marcell Keys Jr.
We love you Baby Mello!

Kea, My Dear Sweet Kea

If I could take this pen and write you a letter in Heaven
That I was positive you'd get a chance to read
I wouldn't write one line about what I want
Not one line about what I need
I wouldn't write about how much I've cried
About how much I miss you so
I wouldn't write about these things at all
Because these things I know, you already know

I wouldn't write about how I long to hear your voice
Passionately engaged in poetic recitation
With great force, power and conviction
And not a hint of hesitation
It's frustrating not to, but I won't write any of that
Because I know it really won't make me feel any better
So Kea, my dear sweet Kea
I decided to write you a congratulatory poem/letter

First and foremost informing you
That we are all okay
We have rested in the fact
That God called you home that Friday
We understand you had to answer His call
Because when a parent calls
That's what good children do
And to simply say you were a good child
Would not be sufficient for you

God put us on this earth to complete a purpose
And He doesn't call us home
Until that purpose is complete
Kea, my dear sweet Kea
You consistently brought love and happiness
To ever person you had an opportunity to meet
By just simply entering a room
And beaming that gorgeous smile
And flashing those big white teeth
You touched people beneath the surface
You touched us way down deep
The traits that came so easily to you
Brought light to many dark days
You had an uncanny ability to change the atmosphere
With the funny and warm things you'd say
Because you were genuine, caring and compassionate
And you showed it in every way
To be absent from the body is to be present with the Lord
So congratulations my dear sweet niece
For making it to those pearly gates
I love you dearly
…Rest in peace

In Loving Memory of my beautiful niece
Ackea Mishawn Davis

1 Man Can Make 1 Woman Hate All Men

Hate has overcome her

She can love no more

Memories of abuse is all she has

She tries with all her might

But just can't forget her past

Now the new man in her life

Is very different you see

But she is no longer herself

She has assumed a new identity

Don't love, don't trust

Is how she feels she should be

If I don't love him

He can't hurt me

The other man messed up

But the new man had to pay

Her distance and coldness

Led him astray

For he truly loved her

And she loved him just the same

But she let her past dictate her future

Now who should take the blame?

Bottled Up & Blue

Is your life in disrepair?
Heart in deep despair?
Don't know how to deal with your emotions
So you act like you don't care?
When people are angry & mean all the time
Trust me…It's deeper than the surface
Deep down inside they desire to change
But can't quite convince *themselves* they're worth it
Changing is the hardest thing to do in this world
And they have grown comfortable with who they are
So nervous & paranoid about change
They act out the pain but hide the scar

They're too scared to experience something different
Search high and low for strength to maintain
Mentally and emotionally they have no control
And still can't figure out what's causing this pain

Pain from a hidden wound
Is the worse pain to go through
In all essence you have no idea what's going on
No idea of what you should do
Walking around tense, aggravated, agitated
Bottled up and blue
No one knows what wrong
…Not even you

Self-Hate Is the Worst Hate

Hurting people doesn't make you a man
Knowing how to love them does
You're trying to figure out what happened to your love
When in all actuality
Your love never was
You hate yourself so you lash out at others
And you don't even know why
You can't do right by those who love you
No matter how hard you try

Self-hate is the worse hate

You spend countless days inflicting pain
Innumerable days wreaking havoc
Destroying those you claim to love
With brutality and malice
But constantly profess your love
As if it's going out of style
If I had a dollar for every time I heard it
This hellish life I live with you
Might be more worthwhile

Self-hate is the worse hate

It's not my intention to be mean
I'm just expressing how I feel
Cut the bull & stop frontin'
…Let's keep it real

You never knew love and love never knew you
And if real love ever came around again?
…You'd destroy that too!
Because a leopard can't change its spots
Just as what comes out of you is from your heart
It's difficult to build a stronger love
While tearing that love apart

Self-hate is the worst hate
I'm sure the least of us would agree
Why not do something about our situations
Instead of living in misery
We can't allow the past to permanently cripple our future
By perpetuating the demise of our mental health
We must overcome the holds of ignorance & complacency
And realize
…Love can only start with self

Why Me?

Sometimes it seems as if bad times
Are all there will ever be
Just when I think I've found my soul mate for life
He turns and runs away from me
How could it be that it's over so soon?
The bitterness has started to consume
My happy song has become a sad tune
And these moist eyes could fill a room

As love has not yet escaped us
And we still have our foundation
Which is trust
Because this relationship was based on love
Not lust
I think getting back together
Is a must

Reality creeps in
With the realization that all things are indefinite
And nothing but death is for eternity
But thoughts of all the good I do for everyone else
Won't allow me to stop wondering

Why me?

But

I get more attention from passersby
Than I do in this place we call home
It's like I don't exist
But you're being wronged?

You treat me like a slut
Scream, holler and talk to me like I'm trash
But I'm being rash?

It's crazy when everyone wants me
Everyone except the one I'm with
I sleep alone every night
Never touched, never kissed
But I'm not supposed to be pissed?

My days are short and my nights are long
Just can't figure out where we went wrong

I'm lonely…You're content
You're elated…I'm pissed
I'm aggravated…You're in sheer bliss
What type of foolery is this?

But my butt!!!
Happiness can't rescue me
…If I don't detach myself from misery!

Lonely

Lying here awake thinking only of you
Feeling so all alone
So lonely, so blue
You left me a long time ago
Not physically but mentally
Now I sometimes wonder
If we were really meant to be
We were young and in love
Together all the time
Back then I truly thought
You'd forever be mine
But now it's hard to say
Because things have really changed
I no longer feel comfortable around you
I feel so awkward, so strange
If it were only like it used to be
I know this could last
But I can't hang on to yesterday
I can't dwell in the past
As I sit and think about my future
I try to imagine it without you
It doesn't seem quite right
I'm trying to figure out what to do
You've changed so very much
I guess that's just a part of growing
But you slowly pushed me away
It seems without even knowing

Solitude and depression have become your life
I'm only included when it's convenient
Sometimes you say you don't love me
Do you really mean it?
I know I could never change things back
To the way they used to be
That part of our life is gone forever
We've lost it don't you see?
But we've made it through things before
Things way worse than this
I'm sure we can work it out
But can't help but think about everything we've missed
I'm writing these words from my heart
I wish you could see how I feel
The way you treat me really hurts
I'm beginning to doubt your love is real
If these words ever reach your ears
I hope you know I'm sincere
I think about this all the time
Breaking up is what I fear
I guess men don't realize words hurt
They hurt just as much if not more than what you do
Words can leave a person scarred for life
They can really have an effect on you
In conclusion what I'm trying to say is
If you love someone communicate
In most cases if you wait to try
When you do try it might be too late

Tomorrow is not promised…Why be lonely today?

Truth Is

Truth is… They're together but the union is rough
She never knew anyone she hated this much
He can't stand her either, so they barely ever touch
All hope of happiness together
Has pretty much been crushed

Truth is…Every word spoken results in a fight
Words of encouragement aren't comprehended right
Communication broke down years ago
Exactly when this happened neither of them knows

Truth is…Accusations of infidelity are commonplace
The slightest innocent glance is thrown in her face
Life is too short to waste it on you
I've given all I have and now I'm through

Truth is…The matter has been settled
Feels like I sold my soul to the devil
As I shovel dirt on what's left of this mess
I bury my heartache, pain and stress

Truth is…Tomorrow is as foreign as Mars
But better than living life behind these bars
Afraid to speak because of what might occur
Bottled up to the point my life's a blur

Truth is…I know why the caged bird sings
She sings because she knows one day freedom will ring
And one day she'll spread her wings and fly high
I sing too, because one day…So will I

It Is What It Is

You say you wanna talk
But really you don't
I ask you to keep it real
But you won't

So you tell me what I'm supposed to do
Waste the rest of my life trying to get through to you?
I'm desperately reaching out to a love that's non-existent
I'm trying to figure out where we went wrong
But I must have missed it

We used to cuddle on the couch
But now I cuddle alone
We used to talk on the phone all day
Now I hate to dial your phone
And when you call mine, I roll my eyes
Because another dumb argument, I despise

When did we lose that spark that kept our fire burning?
When did we give up on our love story?
And stop the pages from turning?

I'm learning more and more that it's just not meant to be
Your bags are packed daily but you have yet to leave
Constantly pulling on the strings of my heart
With all these tricks up your sleeve
Brother please…Just leave!

It's Hard to Pull the Trigger

As I bang my head into this wall repeatedly
It hurts but I can't seem to stop
Blood is dripping everywhere, my head is swollen
My stomach is tied in knots
I have a gun in my hand
I'm squeezing the trigger
But this thing just won't move
Sick and tired of the ups and downs
The attitudes and bad moods
Why can't I pull this trigger?

Let me count the days that I've screamed out in pain
Sometimes I feel like I'm going insane
I can't see the sunshine God has for me
Because I brought in this rain
When I chose this abusive man
Who doesn't even know why he's hurting me
Apparently he has issues he can't even see
Meanwhile, my lip is busted, three ribs are broken
And I have two black eyes
Slowly realizing what I found in my crackerjack box
Really wasn't a prize
Why...Can't I pull this trigger?

As I assess the value of this useless relationship
My heart skips three beats
Despair begins to creep into my soul
I feel like I want to go to sleep

As he spits in my face, tells me I'm useless
And screams I can't do anything right
My body is weak from loss of blood
I have no strength left to fight
So I lie down on the bed and close my eyes
I pull gun up to my head and again I squeeze
But the trigger still won't slide
Why can't I...Pull this trigger?

I'm rolling with the punches
Ducking and dodging, bobbing and weaving
Desperately trying to avoid direct blows
The last time he spewed his hate
I forgot to protect my face
As hard as I try to hide it; it still shows
Who knows how long this round will last
Try as I may, this trigger won't move
I'm desperately trying to put him in my past
All I can see is this stain on my shirt
Right where my heart used to be
A thick red stain remains
Where my heart was ripped out
I want to express my pain
But I'm in too much pain to shout
I'm dying...
Why can't I pull...This trigger?

This is how I'm dying
I'm dying to survive
I can't live this way anymore
I'm losing my will to stay alive
Why...Can't...I...Pull...This...Trigger?

Click…Click…Boom!
Finally I muster the strength to pack my bags and leave
But to my surprise I have company
Anger and bitterness left with me too
And I can't get them off me!

The poem you're reading is a symbolic contrast
Of physical and emotional abuse
In this specific situation a punch was never thrown
However, the emotional abuse inflicted was just as profuse
Some say emotional abuse is not as bad as physical
I'm a testament it's not true
Let's be real, bruises heal
But abusive words
Hang around way longer than the bruises do
Words cut like a knife and although there's no blood
The scars left behind are very real
And to the abused, the absence of a punch
Doesn't make the pain any harder to feel

By no means is this victim suicidal
The gun is simply a metaphor
It symbolizes leaving an unhealthy relationship
Pulling the trigger is simply walking out the door
Sticks and stones may break my bones
But words will never hurt me
Is one of the biggest lies ever told
If we change our mindsets
And seek help for our issues
The cycle of abuse will unfold!

Someone please break this cycle!!!

Gone Is the Light of Day

Chained to a corpse like slaves on a ship
Not a quick plummet…But a gradual slip
Hopelessly entangled in thistles and thorns
Never to remain the same forever shattered and torn
Outlook no longer bright and shiny
But now battered and worn
Praying in desperation to outlive this storm
Slowly being removed from reality
No longer able to resist gravity
Going down hard like the Titanic
No time to brace…Skip right to the panic
Constantly being sucked into a dark, negative, gloomy abyss
If relief is anywhere around it has surely been missed
Entwined in despair and soaked in sorrow
Desperately hoping to never see tomorrow
Simplicity woven into the most intricate knot
It's easier to figure the ballistics by hand
After a loved one has been shot
Roaming the portals of the mind
In a desperate search for peace
Clawing for the surface
But remaining underneath
Head cloudy like the marine layer
Creeping in on the California coast
A feeling that couldn't be emptier if it resided in a ghost
The most loving days are those spent alone
Homeless in spirit because no place feels like home
A gross loss of hope
An unyielding sense of worthlessness
MAYDAY, FLARE SIGNALS, SOS, HELP
And any other alert for distress
Praying for more
But only expecting less…Gone is the light of day!

What About Me?

Continuously bending
Constantly adjusting
Neglecting self
Denying me
When anyone needs anything I come running
Who's going to run for me?

Who's going to cater to my needs?
Feed my desires?
Think about lifting me at all
While I'm lifting them higher?
At some point reciprocity must exist
Someone has to pencil me in on their list

What about me?

The trials of a relationship
Are as hard as a battle of war against the worst enemy
And retreat is sometimes the only wise move
An unhealthy relationship
Eats away at each individual like cancer
If you stay in it without working
Both of you will lose

There are three vital elements in a relationship:
Love, Trust and Respect
The relationship suffers when they're replaced by
Anger, Bitterness and Neglect
Years later you end up lonely on a quest to find yourself
Trying to heal your wounds and replenish your health
Feeling utterly lonely asking…
What about me?

I'm soul searching now on that quest to find me
Being lost in someone else for an extended period of time
Helps you lose sight of your own identity

How do you journey alone?
When you've journeyed with someone else for so long?
How do you sing "Me, Myself & I"
When "Just the two of us" has been your song?

My hopes, dreams & aspirations have either
Diminished greatly or completely disappeared
How do you journey on separate roads
...Very far apart?
When you've spent years on the same road with another
...Very close, very near?

Each day offers a brand new opportunity of confusion
A fresh chance to stay caught up in love's illusion
Another possibility you'll run back to what you know
To that same solitude and loneliness
That wouldn't allow you to grow

The smoke has cleared and I'm standing all alone
...Now focusing on me!

PHASE 2

Emotional Roller Coaster

Excuse Me While I Find Myself

"Not forgiving someone is like drinking poison and
expecting the other person to die!"
—John L. Bowen Sr.

A great deal of what should have been my developmental years was spent coping and adjusting. In the aftermath of the abuse, I didn't know who I was as a person. As I searched my mind, I couldn't even tell myself what my ambitions and aspirations were. I didn't have any values, no morals, and I barely knew what I liked and disliked. My emotions took hold and "finding Dani" became a fierce up-and-down, side-to-side ride that frightened me with every twist and turn. I was on an emotional rollercoaster desperately sifting through the pain...In search of myself. Needless to say, this rollercoaster had many stages.

The rollercoaster of masking the pain:
    In the aftermath of the pain, I stood all alone. I was desperately trying to tape and glue the pieces of my broken life. Even when the sun was shining as bright as it could, I remained in a dark place. The core of me was confused, angry, bitter, and hopeless. However, I perfected masking the pain by burying it deep down inside. I became successful in hiding it from the world and everyone in it. I walked around every day with a fake smile that said "all is well" to everyone who viewed it. I buried the abuse so deep I lost any memory of most of it ever occurring. The reality of this hidden abuse hit me like a ton of bricks when it came back in the form of horrible nightmares. I didn't want to face the reality of those dreams, so I trained my body not to sleep. I robbed my body of its required and much-needed rest for many years. Finally, sleep deprivation began to take its toll on me. It became difficult to wear my phony smile and to act as if all was well. My mood changed severely and when I looked in the mirror, I saw the foul person I thought I had gotten rid of.

I feared becoming who I once was. I didn't want to be that mean person who physically lashed out and cut people into a million pieces with my tongue. Therefore, those closest to me witnessed me slowly becoming more withdrawn as the days went by.

The rollercoaster of confusing sex and love:
Sadly, this rollercoaster was a product of not only what was inflicted upon me but also what I had inflicted upon myself. My dad taught me and constantly reminds me, "Never make decisions based on emotions." Had I learned this simple yet valuable information early on in life, I would have saved myself a whole lot of heartache. Still stuck in the love is sex façade, I repeatedly banged my head into the same walls and desperately hoped for different results. Of course by definition…This was insanity. Needless to say, my search for different results came up null and void. Choices are ours to make but we often fail to realize the results of those choices are owned by us as well. However, those past situations and relationships were definitely the fuel responsible for burning the fire inside the woman I am today. Each and every situation taught me how to value myself and forced me to take the power away from sex and any man who is seeking it from me. Now, I have the power! You learn as you live and if you learn the right things…You live better!

The "rain, rain, go away" rollercoaster:
Scripture tells us it rains on both the just and the unjust. Therefore, this journey we call life will certainly bring in clouds that will unleash rain. You can rest assured we will all experience drizzles of rain, light to moderate showers, and even heavy rainfall that will

momentarily block any hope of ever seeing the sun shining again. Whatever the forecast may be, it's unrealistic that we cease to exist.

One day while contemplating giving up on everything, I studied my life and saw a pattern. No matter how bad it seemed, no matter how hard it rained, eventually the sun would begin shine. Over and over again, when I thought I couldn't stand another drop of rain…the sun came to my rescue. It had been a vicious cycle but in the end, the sun prevailed. Since this realization, whenever I felt like I was in a downward spiral, I was able to recognize it. My course of action was to either change that particular course of events or hold on for dear life until God brought in the sunshine. It was the weirdest thing. I actually had some control over what happened in my life. If I didn't want to do something, I could actually say no to someone and not feel guilty. If I wanted to do something that others disagreed with, it didn't matter what they thought about it. I realized this was my life and I was responsible for the outcome! I realized I could endure the rain simply because I knew the sun would eventually shine again! I realized I didn't have to be a victim; I could be a victor! In essence, I realized life was worth living!

The rollercoaster of forgiveness:
Forgiveness was a foreign concept to me. How do you forgive? What is forgivable? Why should I forgive? People had wronged me and I had every right to hold that against them. I had a right to hold on to the "woe is me" mentality that ruled my existence. I had all the

answers and forgiveness wasn't a possibility. What I failed to realize is that my unforgiving spirit wasn't helping me but it was a hindrance to me and all I hoped to accomplish. I can hear my dad's voice telling me, "Forgiveness is not for the other person...It's for you!" Eureka! That was it! I had been mentally torturing myself by refusing to forgive. All while the people I refused to forgive had moved on with their lives and I was still stuck. My refusal to forgive was blocking the path to my own freedom. I couldn't continue to walk around angry with these people. As long as I did, they would continue to hold me in bondage and also keep the keys to my freedom. I had been held back for too long and I was ready to deal with any and everything that threatened the freedom I desired. I have since then faced the demons of my past and I can say with a sincere heart...I have forgiven each and every one of them.

In the end, my emotional rollercoaster resulted in a woman who developed the ability to overcome abuse and pain. She emerged from the darkness with strength she had never before experienced and determination to successfully continue her journey of life. Although I felt a sense of freedom, I didn't feel as if I were totally liberated. I still had this nagging feeling that there was more freedom to be found...

Dangerously Obscured Reality

Sometimes I feel as if I am…
Traveling at a high rate of speed in the wrong direction
On a one-way street
My eyes are open
And I'm cognizant of the fact that there's danger
But my mind is not fully engaged in the trouble I seek
And I speak from a place of confusion
Ridiculed in shame, soaked in despair
Maligned in pain, even blood stained
I know…It's insane
I feel like Dorothy, there's no place like home
But this is difficult
Because I'm not entirely sure where I belong
So if I click these heels, Kansas might evade me
And I could end up in a place just as wrong
If not worse…So why bother?
You see, my mind already sees things as they should be
Not even close to what they really are
It takes me to a place of peace…A world of tranquility
Very far away from my reality of hostility
Its killing me, Real…Real…Slow like
I guess I'm similar to a fiend who shoots dope up her arm
She knows it's not good
And would be the first to admit
In the long run the high is not worth the harm
So why do I continue to engage
In that which is detrimental to me?
That which causes my heart further pain?
That which has the ability to take me out the game?
I'm glad you asked, cause that…I don't know!
My reality is dangerously obscured

What You See Isn't Necessarily Reality

Don't get it twisted
What you see isn't necessarily reality

This woman that seems to fly high
Is actually being choked by gravity
The proof is in the pudding
…You don't have to wonder
And I must insist, you not judge a book by its cover

You say she's lucky; she has it all?
Pssh…Not at all
She appears to be pseudo-sophisticated
But in reality she's perpetrating a fraud

She smiles for your cameras
And waits for your applause
Her days are lonely
At night she cries all alone in her bed
Finally getting all the built up
Hurt & frustration out of her head
You see she walked around all day
With a phony smile and a warm disposition
When all along she wanted to scream
Or better yet just come up missin'

Your reality of her planet is an illusion
The happy life you assume she has
Is riddled with confusion
You've interrupted her happy façade with your intrusion
Your reality further adds to her torment

Your expectations, hope and the things you mention
However, she clearly understands
Trials and tribulations are designed to strengthen
So your reality will help her get things into perspective
To understand love is the opposite of feeling rejected
One day she'll have enough courage
To rid her life of this sorrow
But for now she'll just wake up tomorrow
Wash yesterday's tears from her face
And replace them with today's famous painted smile
She knows this cover up will only last for a little while
Only those who possess a special gift
Of observation will see

Don't get it twisted
…What you see isn't necessarily reality

Alone

All alone on the edge
This pain and misery I dread
Looking all around for a ledge
Or anything to put piece of mind in my head

All alone on the street of solitude
Wondering why I'm being misused
Men suck up your love as if it's food
And won't show an ounce of gratitude

All alone on the verge of tears
Thinking of all the deception through the years
Scared to open my heart or let him near
But I know I can conquer my fears

All alone in the midst of the madness
Beat down and abandoned
Happiness has been consumed
And I've generated sadness
But as strong as the hold is
I know I can get past it

All alone on the Bayou of defeat
Searching for a way to conquer this feat
Anything is better than retreat
I'm giving it to God and waiting for him to speak

Not Again!

Slowly sinking back into the lonely solitude
That once held my soul
Desperately searching for an answer of contentment
But just can't find control
A few weeks ago I was slowly slipping
But now I'm plummeting fast
Back into the dark, ugly arms of depression
I pray my sanity lasts

I'm losing that firm grasp I have on reality
Because I've held it for so long
My hands are throbbing with aches and pains
I don't know how much longer I can hold on
There's so much going on in my life
I don't know what to straighten out first
It never fails my decision is backwards
What I chose to leave for last is the worst

Why is my life so complicated?
Does it have to be this way?
I wish I could find true happiness
Most of all, I wish it would stay
Tears stream down my face
As anger and hurt boil inside
I really should get out of here
But there's nowhere to run and hide

Please oh please…Not again!

Conquer the Madness If You Can

Reaching, feeling, lurking, seeking
For
Understanding, compassion, commitment & to getherness
But only finding
Rejection, torment, ridicule and pain
Which makes me feel
Devastated, humiliated and betrayed
Slowly feeling
Let down, set aside, thrown away and misused
Gradually becoming
Hard, cold, mean, nasty and vengeful
Trying hard not to let these feelings take over
But my innards are on an up rise
I can feel the turmoil boiling inside
Uprising to the highest peak
An up rise much like:
The Mandingo warrior
Who has been hit one too many times
By the slave master's whip
He tries to hold back
But his anger is starting to slip

An up rise much like:
The very tall, beautiful black stallion
Who has been ridden too hard for too long
It was once tamed
But now it can't fight to urge to do wrong
An up rise much like:
The innocent youth of 15
Who has been dealt a bad hand all his life

And decides to turn to violence and evil deeds
And he knows that when he does
He'll give up any chance of his lifelong dream to succeed
However, I am a strong black woman
Who has overcome many things and many more I will
I can't allow my actions to be determined by how I feel
My roots are strong and firmly planted
In self-worth and determination
Therefore I must redirect anger
And allow negativity to become my motivation
Having taught myself the values of life
With a strong will and a good mindset
I believe I can conquer all
I know what I need to do
Even though I'm not quite ready to make that call
I must overcome these feelings
Of desolation, distrust and hate
For if not, I've already determined not only my fate
But the fate of my seeds
I brought them to this ugly world
Just as my mother brought me
Rather than leave them to figure out
This, huge, crazy, mixed-up world and life alone
I will be there with them
Guiding, protecting, nurturing, teaching
And most of all loving them
Til' death do we part
Thinking in this mind state has calmed me
And put me in a better position to react
I feel
Relaxed, renewed, rejuvenated, refreshed
Restored and serene
Able to conquer all things

Who Cares What They Say?

They called me rat attack because my clothes had holes
The anguish this caused my already troubled world
…Only God knows
They laughed and talked about me
When I came to school smelling like pee
They didn't know the water was off
I couldn't pay the bill, so that wasn't on me
They said I was bald headed & my hair was nappy
And silly little me…LOL!
I thought I needed their approval to be happy
They laughed at me in their circles
And when I tried to play with them they scoffed
Eventually the only emotion I had was pissed off
A rage burned deep down inside
And soon I exploded in a sudden eruption
This set a course that shook my life with hostile abruption
If I could go back and grab the little girl I was
I'd say, "Why do you care?"
"Don't allow them to take you there"

Who cares what they say?

Some will always look at me
As that small timid, dirty, nappy-headed little girl
Who was too scared to stand up for herself
And therefore remained timid before the world
But here I stand a full grown woman
Who holds her head up high
Who is intimidated by no one and fears only God
Now tears of joy are the only tears her eyes cry

She takes pride in her appearance, but isn't vain
She remembers the heartache of the past
But knows in it, her destiny is not contained
She thanks God for her difficult past
With all the dark clouds and rain
Then she shouts as she thanks Him
For the strength He placed deep within her to sustain

Who cares what they say?

You see they talked about me when I was less fortunate
And they still talk about me
Now that I'm fortunate to have a little bit
I just can't seem to get away from
The attacks of insecure misfits
Now they say my hair is too pretty to be real
…It must be weave
They say I think I'm all that
Because my clothes are always pressed and clean
They say I'm stuck up
Because I don't come outside with a rag on my head
Or walk out of the house in the clothes I wear to bed
They say I'm boojee because when I enter a room
My head is held high
Because when they spew their hatred in my direction
I don't run away and cry

Why would I?

Who cares what they say?

…Definitely not me!

Chances Are . . . You Could Be My Hater

Does my assertiveness and confidence offend you?
My refusal to bend for the sake of right upset you?

Chances are…You could be my hater

If you think less of me
Because I won't conform
To your shiesty way of doing things
Because I have morals
And don't want the trouble it brings

Chances are…You could be my hater

If I have never personally wronged or harmed you
But the mere mention of my name
Puts a bad taste in your mouth

Chances are…You could be my hater

Does the smile on my face
Make you itch in an unusual way?
The fact that my head is always held high
Just ruin your day?

Chances are…You could be my hater

If I've never bumped into you in a crowded room
Or stepped on your shoe
Or caused you to lose money
Or verbally insulted you
Or pushed you down

Or slapped your face
Or put dirt on your name
If I've never exposed your dirt
Thus causing you shame
But you still roll your eyes when I enter a room
And your prayer for me
Is that I will soon meet my doom?

Chances are…You could be my hater

If my success makes your skin crawl
And you spit at the thought of my existence
But you can't say what I did to you
You have no examples of my wrongdoings
Not one, for instance

Chances are…You could be my hater

But I'm not mad
I love my haters
Like the army they encourage me to be all I can be
They fuel my fire
And help bring out the best in me
As much as I hate to displease my haters
Displease you, I must
You see, I have planted my roots in excellence
And of course in God I trust

Haters give me drive with their constant attention
Did I mention?
My haters helped me get two college degrees
They did that when they said I would never succeed

That I'd always be a high school dropout
Working dead-end jobs and collecting welfare
When they gossiped in their circles…As if I care
I would be the last to toot my own horn
But rather the first to pat you on the back
For helping put my life into prospective
For keeping me on the right track

I am far from perfect
I still have flaws that sometimes hinder me
They're just not on the surface
For the entire world to see

So I'm sorry to report
Who I am is not up for debate
But who you are should be
Before it's too late
You spend so much time worrying about me
Your life is in disarray
If that same energy was spent on yourself
…You'd be more productive at the end of the day

Haters take a bow!

Where Did That Love Go?

Untouched & unloved
Unappreciated & undervalued

Unadulterated & downright stone cold neglect
Unprotected & Unashamed
Too close to wild to be tamed

I slowly released my grip on reality
Abandoning myself to the sheer bliss of my fantasies
They calmed me & quieted my fears
Gave me an alternate love to be near
A love that would hold me and never let me go
This love is the love I used to know

Sensitive & sincere
Pleasant & pure
Construct & concrete
Tender & true
Mature & meaningful
Where did that love go?
…The love I used to know!

My Journey Does Not End Here

As a child I was told I was intelligent
And I could be anything I wanted to be
I strayed away for a while
But I returned to my education
Because success was instilled in me

Mama constantly told me the sky was my limit
But I chose to travel down a narrow road
I got pregnant at 16 and dropped out of school
Which sets the stage for this story to unfold

Through blood, sweat and tears, I've struggled for years
God held my hand, and calmed my fears
My journey *does not* end here

At 18, I gave birth to my second son
And soon realized something wasn't quite right
Dead-end jobs were getting us nowhere
So to get my GED
I studied day and night

In three short months I had my diploma
And off to college I went
Then a year and a half in, I dropped out again
Because I needed a second job to pay the rent

Through blood, sweat and tears, I've struggled for years
God held my hand, and calmed my fears
My journey *does not* end here

So I'm working these two jobs, and raisin' these two kids
And it's hard because I feel like I'm all alone
My current relationship was stressful & very disrespectful
I had to let that go because it was all wrong
So I run into an old friend and at 23 I'm pregnant again
And once again my education is postponed

Hold up, wait a minute…

I don't want you to get me wrong, I love my kids
But if I could do it again
This story & poem would be different
Though they never missed a meal,
The thought lingers still
To be able to provide more?
I'd do it differently in an instant

Through blood, sweat and tears, I've struggled for years
God held my hand, and calmed my fears
My journey **does not** end here

A year after I give birth to my daughter
We set off on a journey to Minnesota
Because I feel like I'm being led in a different direction
But little did I know, what God had in store
Salvation, forgiveness, love, and protection

So now I'm knee-deep in church, being busy for the Lord
I even managed to pick a husband along the way
He tells me I'm too smart not to be in school
And to stop putting off for tomorrow
What I should do today

Through blood, sweat and tears, I've struggled for years
God held my hand, and calmed my fears
My journey **does not** end here

So I put on my ridin' boots and jumped back in the saddle
Aiming for the top and not taking anything less
I put in mad study hours, way into the night
Because I was dead set on being the best

I graduated Phi Theta Kappa
And received my Associates degree
Two years later I received my Bachelor's
The devil in hell can't stop me

So if there is something you want to do in this life
But don't have the courage to see it through
I say to you, don't think just do it
Take that first step to becoming a better you

Through blood, sweat and tears, I've struggled for years
God held my hand, and calmed my fears
And my journey *will not* end here

All I Got Is Me

When I needed self-esteem
I looked around and it was nowhere to be found
So I invented a brand just for me
Sucked up the pain and held my head up high
For all the world to see
When I needed a pat on the back, I faced facts
The only way that would happen
Is if I suddenly became double-jointed
So sick and tired of being disappointed
By so-called friends and next of kin
Just plain sick and tired and I want it all to end
When I needed encouragement I came to realize
I am the only person who cares enough about me
To encourage me when things are on the right track
Instead of being there for me only
When things are in disarray
Then using my shortcomings to stab me in the back
I need some genuine people in my life…not jealous hearted
I need some "celebrate life" people
I have too many there for "dearly departed"
When I needed a kind smile or an outburst of laughter
Not those consumed with doom and gloom
But happily ever after
One who would not only cry with me, but laugh with me as well
And only these joys & triumphs is what they would run & tell
I soon realized the people I knew
Were only available when I was going through hell
When I needed strength, truth, commitment & dedication
No one ever had any to give, so I finally got tired of waitin'
No more drowning in self-pity and hesitation
I had to open my eyes and see…All I got is me!

A Little Somethin' Somethin'

A little bit of this
A little bit of that
A little somethin' somethin'
To keep me on track
Slack won't get it
Neither will acceptance
A little somethin' somethin'
To keep me from stressin'
Countin' blessings before they arrive
Helps keep me alive
I strive for betterment
My end game is to survive

A little bit of courage
A little bit of grace
A little somethin' somethin'
To keep worry lines out my face
I refuse to allow my past to dictate where I'm going
No defeated life for me
A little somethin' somethin'
To make those demons flee
Walking into newness as if I owned it from day one
Heavily concentrated on winning
My mind firmly set on my end
Being greater than my beginning

A little bit of aggression
A little bit of determination
A little something' something'

To help me avoid hesitation

To conquer every goal set
I charge forward like a lion
A little somethin' somethin'
I'll never stop tryin'
I must defeat every obstacle
I must pass every test
There will be nothing but greatness when I do
My future is blessed

A little bit of this
A little bit of that
A little somethin' somethin'
To keep me on track
A little somethin' somethin'
Has the power to make dreams come true
So find your little somethin' somethin'
No one can stop you...But you!

Can I Have Your Attention Please?

As I walked by he told me I'm beautiful
I flung my hair back and flashed a wide smile
This I already knew
          …I just hadn't heard it in a while
You see at home
I'm appreciated but often ignored
It's as if my mate is simply content and bored

Although my confidence remains strong
I still yearn for attention
For affection, tender love & care
For compliments
          ...Did I mention?
I'm lonely most nights
And my feet are always cold
Sometimes I forget I'm loved
Because despair has taken hold

But I bounce back quickly
Because our love is grounded
Then here comes despair again
I can't seem to get around it
Selective attention makes me itch
I wish and I pray for a better predicament
But since this is what I have
For now, I'll make the best of it

Attention please can I…Have?

If I had to plead for your attention once more
I'd gladly do it
Here it is my final shot
I hope I can keep your attention through it

Can I please have the concentrated direction of your mind?
Touch me!
I've forgotten how the shivers feel
When your fingers trace my spine

Can I please have your consideration, notice & observation?
Look at me!
I really miss your care & concern
Your pampering & dedication

Can I please have your interest indicating affection & love?
Please hold me in your arms
For old time's sake
…Just because

You have no idea what snuggling with you does
It gives me pause and brings me to my knees
Can I have your attention please?

A word to the wise: Pay attention!

I Won't Be Broken

Wounded by harsh words that cut like a knife
High-pitched shrieks and screams
Desperately seek to take my life
Gnashing of teeth
Your words gouge deeply each day
Anger and frustration in every word you throw my way
I really should leave
Yet, for some odd reason I stay

But...I won't be broken

Bruised by disrespect
Cheated on and lied to
Intimidation is rampant
I just can't stand it
Choked off my feet for speaking the truth
Accused repeatedly without reason or proof
Strangled by the hands of oppression belonging to men
Who don't want me to have a voice
...I have a choice
My identity stripped down so bare I feel naked
Expected to just lie down and take it
But me, I fake it til' I make it

Because...I won't be broken

Neglected as if my feelings don't count
I've gone 20 rounds and I'm still ready for the next bout
Always second in line for your time
Only touched to fulfill your needs
My heart was ripped out years ago and still it bleeds
Shattered by years of extra wear and tear
Because I've attached myself to people who don't care
My heart has been shredded
It's been repeatedly taped and glued
I lick my wounds and change my blown fuse

Oh no...I won't be broken

The very essence of my being is a stranger to me
Who I really am is a faded memory
But I'm a clown
I mask the pain inside and maintain a happy face
I put on a show for the people and I stay in my place
So even while the war rages inside my head
On the outside I appear to be happy and care free
But inside I feel dead
Chaotic days and nights
Should have me clinically depressed
I'm perplexed and I'm stressed
...A complete and utter mess

Still...I won't be broken

Am I Ready for Love?

The warm touch of your fingertips
The loving succulent kiss from your lips
The affectionate embrace when you grab my hips
Oooooh someone help me! I'm whipped!
My body is ready but is my mind equipped?

Am I ready for love?

As your finger slowly & softly
Traces the nape of my neck
And enters my spine
My body starts to shiver
I can feel the explosions
Way deep down inside

Am I ready for love?

As you take me into your arms
I can't help but notice
The gentleness in your touch
As you caress every inch of my body
With care & admiration
I realize why I love you so much

Am I ready for love?

Faint sounds of our love making
Can be heard throughout the night
Long, soft kisses & the heartfelt embraces
Of two in love
Make this journey feel right
…But am I ready for love?

Sometimes You Have to "CUT" It Out

This mental strain on my brain
Is driving me insane
So much, I can't maintain
My main objective should be to change my thoughts
So I sought and I fought to do so
But a more intense pain this brought
I was caught up in a most peculiar way
I got down on my knees to pray
It felt good
So I decided to stay and weigh
The costs against the benefits
Of this horrible decision I made
Then I lay
Prostrate before the Lord
On Him I cast all my cares
I took your mess to my prayer closet
…And I left it there
Now I'm done with all the misuse
And extra wear and tear
So I'm going under the knife
To have you surgically removed from my heart
I now realize this thing was wrong from the start
Woman enough to say my eyes were blind
And I could not see
Women enough to admit I made a huge mistake
When I gave you…Me

"CUT" IT OUT!

The Tragic Tale of Is and Was

One day Is traded places with Was
And now what Was, no longer Is
It's washed up, finished, over and done with, caput
I'm letting it go, no matter how good it looks

So I say...
Arrevederchi, adios, sayonara, good-bye
I can no longer hold a thought of it
No matter how hard I try

It's a...
Once was, used to be, ex, history, the past
An irrelevant, temporal escapade destined not to last
It has no bearing on the present
Of it I can remember nothing pleasant
Just a buildup of many bitter memories
That seemingly grows vaguer by the minute
I don't like Was and I hate I ever hooked up with it
It's was a catastrophe, tragedy, shame, disgrace
That Is, set straight and put in its place

What was the issue that broke me down before?
What was final straw that sent me out the door?
What caused this transition to begin?
Dang!...What was ole' boy name again?

Oh yeah, now I remember
Low down dirty dog, Max, Fido, Rover
I'm finally coming back around from this lust hangover

Today's boo will be a figment of tomorrow
If boo don't get some act right
Cause there's a boo out there somewhere
Who will choose to love rather than fight

New Boo, I warn you
Don't become
Complacent, stagnant, dormant, smug
Or you too will be
Switched, swapped, traded, exchanged
There's a waiting list Boo
…Your replacement can be arranged

Woe unto him who knows not the wrong he does
For he will quickly go from Is…To Was
From under your feet I'll pull the rug
Shut this thang down quick, pull the plug

For one who knows how to
Cherish, honor, love, adore
Keep my best interest in his immediate sights
Alright!
See that's what I'm talking about
Is…Is alright with me
Bump a Was…Give me Is

The tragic tale of Is and Was!

little girl lost . . . Grown Woman Found

If I could just take this time to run inside and hide
From the side of my life, I don't wanna see
Could it possibly be, this trickery and mockery
Has deceived me so long I can't see clearly?

I wanna run away and stay away
From the games life loves to play
Begging anyone to lead the way
Anxiously waiting for that day

But my inner woman overcomes doubt
And speaks out in a loud shout
What is this all about?
Retreat ain't the way out!

Can somebody, anybody explain
The insane pain in my brain
This strain that makes me feel
As if I can't maintain, my emotions?
Am I so caught up in a sincere devotion
That this potion has given me the notion
This is all an illusion?

Confusing the very fiber of my being
Keepin' me from seeing
All I need to see
From being all I need to be
Challenging me to the core
I just can't take no more!

However, I must overcome the battle
Because I've already won
The war's done
I have to be an example to my daughters and my sons
So I'mma get back in the saddle
And straddle this horse called life
So the alarm you can sound, it's so profound
little girl lost...Grown Woman Found

Round up the cattle and giddy up...It's going down
That frown that once lived on the corners of my mouth
It had to move around
It don't live here no mo
Neither do low self-esteem, lack of trust, pity and self-hate
They all tried to ride me but they arrived too late
I set em' all straight
And I can't wait to see the look on life's face
When I give em' back

You see life got me read wrong
Because that sad song that once defined me is gone
And it won't be long
Before I reclaim my throne as a true conqueror in Christ
I now realize,
His plan for my life will suffice
The device the devil thought would work
Is no longer in existence
I swear if you blink you'll miss it
Because in an instant persistence defeated my doubt
I'm sooooo loving this Grown Woman I've found!

Free to Be Me

At first I was overwhelmed
I just knew
I didn't deserve this hell
But then I was
Slapped in the face by reality
It overwhelmed and embarrassed me
And sent me off to a place
A place I'd been to
A few times before
A place from the past
I won't forget anymore
A place where
I'm free to be me
Where I can be anything
I want to be
Free as bird to feel the wind
Flapping beneath my wings
To feel the joy
True life brings
I truly enjoy
This new place I see
Thank you for freeing me!

Defying All Odds

What do you do?
When you want something so bad you can taste it?
And all your upbringing has taught you to do is waste it?
Face it...Your defeat is carved in stone
And every time you try to do better
Something goes terribly wrong
The song that defines you is worse than a sad tune
And happiness can't find its way to you
Because of all the gloom
What do you do?
What could you do?
What should you do?
You ignore the voices that repeatedly scream defeat
You avoid the choices that by design have you beat
Firmly plant your feet on the pavement to success
By detaching yourself from anger, misery and stress
Step out of your comfort zone into that unknown abyss
Push off complacency and prepare for sheer bliss
Dismiss the chains of contentment
And unleash your destiny
Know in your heart your best is yet to be seen
And things that block your vision are only smoke screens
You push through the madness and shoot for the stars
You aim for Pluto...Don't settle for Mars
The scars of your past are just that
Scars of the past
Some obsolete situation too powerless to last
You survived and you have so much more to give
        ...You're here
                    ...You're alive
                                ...So live!

I Refuse

I refuse to spend my life…
Hiding behind a bottle
Or sniffing a thin white line
Chasing the magic dragon
Wasting precious time
You won't find me among the ranks
Of the tranquilizer brigade
Laying around numb, uneventful and in a daze
We all have pain and have struggled in many ways
Felt as if we couldn't go on
Searching for better days
But I'm amazed sometimes
By our tenacity & endurance
Our determination to keep seeing it through
How we continue to move on
Even when we don't know what to do
If you stop & take a moment to think about it
I'm sure you would see it too
It's hard for others to keep you down
The fight is deep within you

I refuse to live my life…
With a chip on my shoulder, being bitter
Because my mama was always drunk
And her husband used to hit her
Because I was talked about at school
And teased for what I didn't have
I understand circumstances
Are often out of our grasp

And that others have situations
That causes them to lash out
I understand everyone deals differently
With frustration and doubt
Why pout about the past when the future is so bright
Why hide it under a bushel
When this dying world needs your light
My victory isn't for me
But for someone who still needs to make it through
I could live life defeated but how will that benefit you?

I refuse to live my life…
Stuck in the mistakes of my past
Or desperately in love with a love that won't last
Or walking around depressed
Because my children were born out of wedlock
Or kicking myself in the butt
Because I sped up my clock
Or wandering aimlessly through life
Because I took a few wrong turns
No, instead I'll use those wrong turns
As important lessons learned
I'll pursue excellence like the champ I am
Never will I bow down to defeat
I choose to take a stand

I refuse to live my life...
Mad at the world
Because a job didn't call me back
I'll just go back to school, get further educated
And make a greater impact
On the lives of our children
And this twisted institution
We call the criminal *justice* system
In which racism is promoted
And justice is nowhere to be seen
In which we are still herded
Like sheep for the slaughter
Guilty even when proven innocent
Wrongfully convicted and demeaned

I refuse to allow you to make me hate me
Because that's just what you'd have me do
If you loved yourself
You'd take your spotlight off me
And put the focus on you

I refuse...And you can too!

This House Is Not My Home

This house is not my home
    You can't make me believe otherwise
I'm sick of phony smiling for the people
    I'm taking off the disguise

I won't be held hostage anymore
    In the chains of complacency and deceit
It's time to embark on a journey to find happiness
    And to embrace the challenges I meet

It's time to bask in the glory God promised me
    And leave all this foolery behind
To commit to becoming a better me
    To self-evaluate and get my own self in line

From one place to another I am moving
    Because in this current place I'm over extended
I tried desperately to work it out here
    But my wants and needs aren't comprehended

It's not only that, trust me...There's no other way
    Rejection, ridicule & torment won't allow me to stay
I pray daily for Him to keep me
    While I'm in this transition
As I embark upon a foreign land
    And face seemingly impossible decisions

With persistence I push forward
　　　With determination I move on
Upon this quest I have to find myself
　　　And when I get there I pray...I'm not already gone

Because this song in my heart
　　　Desperately needs a new verse
And what's worse is if I can't find myself
　　　I'll never quench this thirst
The thirst for happiness & joy in its truest form
　　　I ask Him to give me the strength needed
To weather this storm

So I pray for the peace that passes all understanding
　　　Though my situation is demanding and uncanny
I am standing...On...His...Word
　　　And He confirms

...This house is not my home!

Thank You for the Introduction

Trials and tribulations introduced me to me
        Abandonment and rejection introduced me to me
Harsh words and negativity introduced me to me
        Disappointment and rudeness introduced me to me
Brutality and strife introduced me to me
        Torment and ridicule introduced me to me
Miscommunication & accusations introduced me to me
        Hostility and aggravation introduced me to me
Backstabbers and betrayers introduced me to me
        Tension and pressure introduced me to me
Judgment and loneliness introduced me to me
        Fear and resentment introduced me to me
Confusion and hate introduced me to me
        Fake and phony introduced me to me
Pain and distress introduced me to me
        Multiple failed relationships introduced me to me

…And from the depths of my soul
        I thank you all for the introduction!

PHASE 3

Spiritual Cleansing

By His Stripes... I am Healed

"Thank you Paul, Paul told me to tell you
...I can do all things through Christ who strengthens me."
—John L. Bowen Sr.

To those who know me now, it would be hard to fathom, but in my early years, I didn't believe in God. As a matter of fact, I was almost sure He didn't exist. I can remember having conversations with my brother Donny about God. We would say God couldn't exist because if He did exist, He wouldn't allow us to go through the things we were going through as innocent children. Needless to say, there was a lot missing from those conversations. We didn't know or understand the concept of man's dominion and free will or the concept of depravity. Therefore, you have read several poems in this book in which I doubt and question the very existence of God. After lengthy consideration and a lot of toiling on what to do with these poems I decided to leave them in, as is. I could have easily restructured them or deleted them all together, but they play an integral part in my journey. These poems are a testament to those who still don't believe. It shows that just because you don't see God's intervention, doesn't mean He's not intervening. Now today, I thank my Lord and Savior Jesus Christ for keeping me until I was wise enough to see His hands all over me from day one. I know He kept me and I believe He kept me so I could be a living testimony for Him!

Ironically, as far back as I can remember, I have always felt an indescribable presence. It was as if every time I got to my breaking point, someone or something would intervene and say, "That's enough." Relief would always come at that point, allowing me to come up for air and regroup before the next series of unfortunate events. In addition to the presence, I have always had a thirst for something, and at first, I didn't know what it was. It felt as if I was missing a major part of myself. There was a hole on the inside. A void if you will. A void that couldn't be filled by anything I had ever experienced. The greatest and most complete love I had known up to this point was the love of my children and their love couldn't even fill it. To my astonishment, the second I gave my life to the Lord, the indescribable presence was revealed and the void was filled. I suddenly felt complete. It was as if a burden had been lifted and now I am truly free. I now know that indescribable presence was the Lord. He was right there, holding me in His loving arms the whole time. I am thoroughly convinced He knew me in the womb!

The more I embraced the concept of being Christ-like, the more my life changed. The money I used to use to get my nails done with quickly went into the collection plate as tithes and offering. The violent and sex-filled music I used to listen to was slowly replaced by gospel music. The multitude of curse words that used to fill my everyday language were substituted and then replaced altogether. The slaps, kicks, and punches I used to express my anger were replaced by handshakes and hugs that I now use to express my love. The tongue that I used to tear others down is now used to uplift those I come into contact with. God slowly changed me into a new creation. He has achieved what no one or nothing in this world could ever do. He placed His love and peace in my heart and now I am stronger than I have ever been. I don't know or understand why He chose someone like me...But I'm glad he did! I am over-joyed to be in the unchanging hands of the Father. Never in my life had I experienced true joy; joy that could only come from the Master. Now there is within my members and unexplainable feeling of completeness!

...Jesus is the best thang that's ever happened to me!

Before & After Salvation

Agony & Anger – Agape & Adoration
Bitterness & Bondage – Benevolence & Blessings
Chained & Condemned – Changed & Consecrated
Deceitful & Depraved – Devoted & Delivered
Empty & Envious – Edified & Emancipated
Fearful & Filthy – Forgiving & Faithful
Guarded & Greedy – Gracious & Guided
Hellish & Hostile – Honorable & Holy
Ignorant & Insecure – Inheritance & Intercession
Jealous & Juvenile – Joyful & Justified
Kidnapping & Killing – Knowledge & Kindness
Lewd & Lascivious – Love & Life
Mean & Menacing – Manifestation & Mercy
Neglect & Nuisance – Navigation & New Creation
Oppressed & Opinionated – Outstretched Arms & Obedience
Prisoners & Pain – Pardoned & Paradise
Quick Tempered & Quivering – Quarantined & Quickened
Retribution & Rebellion – Redeemed & Restored
Stubborn & Superficial – Surrendered & Sanctified
Tortured & Tightfisted – Testimony & Tithing
Uncaring & Unworthy – Understanding & Upright
Violent & Vindictive – Veiled & Vindicated
Worthless & Wicked – Washed & Worthy
Xtreme for the world – Xtreme for the Kingdom
Yoked – Yielding
Zero – Zion

One Day I Met a Man

One day I met a man
And he told me everything I needed to hear
Gave me this feeling on the inside
That snatched away every fear
Placed His loving hands on my face
And He wiped away every tear
And I hear
Him softly whispering my name
When temptation comes like a thief in the night
It's waving evil in my face
When I'm trying to do right
But in spite of my faults
He loves me unconditionally
Doesn't have to lift a finger to my enemies
But He makes them flee
Holds me gently when I'm sad
Soothes my anger when I'm mad
And I'm glad to have Him in my life
That He's molding me into a better
Christian, friend, mother and wife

He showed me that I **had** to be destroyed
So that He could rebuild
That I had to **first** be purged in order to be filled
With His precious Holy Spirit, because in an instant
I would be tempted by this misfit the devil
But because He leveled my mind
Satan's not a threat to me
My eyes are now open and I can clearly see
He's my Shepherd and I shall not want
He helped me close the door to my past
And now my dreams don't haunt

He showed me how to take a strong stance
To claim the victory in my life
He took away the bitterness, hurt, pain and strife
Took the power away from the device
People held over my head
And got rid of my feelings
...Of better off dead

Instead
He taught me how not to conform to this world
But to be transformed by the renewing of my mind
And when I slip up and do the things I used to do
He's firm but he's also kind
I find that over time I have aligned my thoughts with His
And the desire to do those things is gone
He cleaned up my speech
And in my heart He put a brand new song
So today as I contemplate my fate, my heart elates
At the realization that this man has wiped my slate clean
I know the worse is over and the best is yet to be seen

You didn't have to take me in
But you did it anyway
I'm eternally grateful for your love
And proudly I say
If I never met Jesus there's no telling where I'd be
Words cannot express my gratitude to Him
For saving a wretch like me
Thank you Jesus!

Seeing is NOT Believing

One day I ignorantly gave God a proposition
You see, I thought I had to do so
In order to reach my decision
I wasn't positively sure He existed
He had already shown me His existence
...But I dismissed it
But now even though I don't understand
How He works
...I know He does
He found me where I was
Broken, bruised and all alone
Used up and abandoned
Like waste into the garbage heap I was thrown
Life threw me like a ship on the raging sea
I was over exposed
Because I thought my body was the key
I was overtly verbal
And shouted expletives without care
I was violent and I used my fists to solve problems
My mind was in bondage
My soul enslaved
He met me where I was
And my standards He raised
He planted me at the corner
Of Grace Avenue and Mercy Boulevard
He easily accomplished what for me was too hard

Now, I no longer trust that which I see
That which my hands can feel
I trust what I've never laid eyes on
I know in my heart that's what's real
I'm no longer interested
In what I can physically view
Give me something I can't explain
Like how He disrobed divinity
Why He loves a wretch like me
How He saved me
Feeds me daily
Clothes my body
How He transformed my worthless life
Unplugged my deaf ears
Made medicine out of mud
And restored my sight
Kept me in my right mind
When I should be stark raving mad
I hooked up with someone
Who gave me something no one else ever had
Eyes have not seen and ears have not heard
I no longer need an explanation
I trust His Word
I have experienced His work in my life
I have felt His touch
I never knew I could love
Someone I've never seen before
…This much

Seeing is NOT believing!

If Only...

My God who is faithful
Came here & gave up His life for you
He came to set men free
Lived a perfect life & still died on Calvary
He healed their sick and raised their dead
But they spit in His face and bruised His head
When flesh was pulled from His body
And the blood began to pour
These same onlookers in the crowd
Cheered and begged for more
They hung Him high & stretched Him wide
Broke not a bone, but pierced His side
Then they buried Him in Joseph's tomb
But began the party all too soon
If only...They knew

My Jesus rose you see
And when He did
He gave the power to you & me
I refuse to allow my past to dictate where I'm going
No defeated life for me
Wise men still seek Him
And when they do they live in harmony
Jesus accepted me into His bosom
He showers me in His kindness
He threw my transgressions into the sea of forgetfulness
Spit in the mud, anointed my eyes
And relieved my blindness
He wrote my name in the Book of Life
And His Word on the tablet of my heart
If only...I'd known the love of Christ from the start

The Spiritual D.N.A Test:

Who's Yo Daddy?

Who's yo Daddy?

Do you give all you can?
Or take all you can get?

Do you remain content when the storm comes?
Or do you lose faith and have a fit?

Do you curse people with your tongue?
Or do you use it to bless?

Do you cast your cares upon Him?
Or do you live defeated by your stress?

Do you encourage your fellow sisters and brothers?
Or do you put one another down?

Do you reach out your hand to those who are troubled?
Or do you stomp them farther into the ground?

Do you actively seek the Lord in your daily life?
Or do you deal with Him only when you're in church?

Do you help the young seek to find their value?
Or do you help further diminish their worth?

Do you honor the sanctity of a marital union?
Or do you cause friction between husbands & wives?

Do you love you neighbor as yourself?
Or do you hate, covet and despise

Who's yo Daddy?

Encouraged

When all that surrounds me is shaky and unstable ground
When I'm beaten and broken
And my way can't be found
I'm encouraged

Though my winds blow hard
And my waves crash into my own sea
I know weeping endureth but a night
Simply means, God got me
I'm encouraged

A strong woman writes these words
And with confidence I say
Many virtuous women have come before us
And with grace they paved the way
I'm encouraged

Adam had everything
But he still wasn't complete without Eve
God knew men needed women
In order to fully succeed ☺
I'm encouraged

Mary gave birth to Jesus
The one who died on Calvary for our sins
And she did it even though she faced ridicule & scorn
From her family & friends
I'm encouraged

The Bible says Mary was blessed because she believed
And because her soul magnified the Lord
Her husband didn't leave
I'm encouraged

Jochebed gave birth to Moses, Aaron and Miriam
And yes she raised them right
She was determined to keep Moses alive
And he lived to put up a fight
I'm encouraged

The Samaritan woman showed us perseverance
That tipped the scale
She also showed us great faith
And if we use it...We won't fail
I'm encouraged

Mary the sister of Martha gave us love and adoration
When she poured perfume on Jesus' feet
Women of God
We should show that same love & adoration
To everyone we meet
I'm encouraged

So like Hagar
I kick these stumbling blocks and clear my path
Resting & trusting solely in the Lord
And not the math
I'm encouraged

The math in my life
Says I should be going to Hell
But the Word of my God says
No weapon formed against me
Will prevail
I'm encouraged

Man says one + one = two
And two + two = fo (LOL)
And that abuse and neglect
Should have stopped me a long time ago
I'm encouraged

But I'mma stand in front of this wicked world
Like Esther stood in front of the king
Casting all my cares on the Lord
Basking in the love He brings
I'm encouraged

Women are precious flowers
They bloom when they believe
So when you look at your situation, I plead
Take hold of the Lord's hand
And follow His lead
Don't believe the hype
You can succeed

Be encouraged!

Carnal vs. Spirit

We've allowed our carnal man
To take control of our souls
This hold has boldly twisted us
We're trapped in an illusion
Confusion consumes us
This carnal man has doomed us
Ashes to ashes, dust to dust
God is the one I trust
He breathes the breathe of life into our nostrils
…exhumes us
Writes His Word on the tablet of our heart
…renews us
Still our spirits say yes
But our flesh says no
Stuck like a deer in headlights
We don't know which way to go
In the Book of Life He wrote our names
Gave us the power to change the game
The Spirit is willing but the flesh is weak
We have to stop listening to this flesh when it speaks

The one you feed the most…Will always be the strongest!

My Pastor

Blessed is the man who is chosen by God
He Himself gave some to be pastors and teachers
God reached way deep down in His bosom
And blessed GMV with one of His best preachers
While he was in the womb God knew him
And He touched him with His mighty hand
That's why his feet are planted so firmly in the gospel

So he can take all our mess and still stand
From the big to the small he handles it all
He stands firm in what he believes
He lets us know the devil has no power
And if we follow the Lord we will succeed
My pastor is a very well-rounded individual
He wears many hats and has many roles
Though I could never name them all
I will name a few
Because the half is yet to be told
He preaches with conviction and an unquenchable fire

This comes from the Holy Spirit
He tells us what thus says the Lord
He prays we will apply it as well as hear it

He teaches better than the best professor
At any of the best Ivy League Schools
He takes his time so we all understand it
That we understand is his first rule
He counsels with an outstretched hand of compassion
Understanding, patience and kindness
He gives us the words of wisdom God gave him

In an effort to lead us out of our blindness
He disciplines with a very firm hand
Full of encouragement and love
He gets his guidance from the one with the master plan
Our Heavenly Father above
I never would have made it
If it had not been for the Lord on my side

Nor if it had not been for the pastor
He gave me as a guide
He's God's warrior
And he simply won't stop until the battle is won
There's no doubt one day he will hear
Thy good & faithful servant well done

Dedicated to my pastor, dad, counselor, teacher,
mentor & much more: Reverend John L. Bowen Sr.

In **God's Answer to the Problem of Pressure** he told us:
Sometimes you need to leave the crowd
And go to a desert place
It's very difficult to reflect with people in your face
They'll have you using an atomic bomb
In a firecracker situation
And the most important thing is to talk to Jesus
While you're on this vacation

In **Who is the Greatest** he said:
Some of us think we're God Jr.
And are as far away from God
As Heaven is from the Earth
We need to put down what we call great
And watch small children
Because this is where we'll find worth

In **Making it on Broken Pieces** he told us:
Sometimes a storm leaves us with broken pieces
And we have to hold on to those pieces to survive
Don't get comfortable and live in the miserable aftermath
But thank Him for being there with us
And that He kept us alive

In **A Praying Church** he said:
Prayer is the foundation of the Christian
It's the only thing the Bible tells us we should always do
Prayer is to the believer as the heart is to the body
For when you're not talking to God
The devil is talking to you

In **He Didn't Bring Us This Far
to Leave Us Now** he told us:
God took the people out of Egypt
And He wanted Egypt out of them
But for some of them it didn't work
We're out of the streets but the streets are still in us
And our Heavenly Father continues
To sift through our dirt

In **What Jesus Wants for Christmas** he said:
Jesus wants us to praise Him, to give all year
And He wants us to go back another way
If we come to church fussing and fighting
Church *should* give us a better end to our day

In **The Devil Came Down from Heaven
to Bring Hell on Earth** he said:
We fall into the wicked traps of the devil
Simply because we don't recognize his strategic plan
He attacks our finances, faith and family
And causes as much destruction as he can

In **How to Stay Spiritually Fit
After You Leave Church** he told us:
Stay in the Word daily and not just on Sunday
For anyone who eats once a week is not fit
Stay out of the world and don't blend in
Then you don't have to blame the devil
For the trouble you get

In **A Dead Situation** he said:
Sometimes God lets our Lazarus die
So he can introduce Himself
But we don't roll our stone away
Because we missed the link
Expecting God to do everything for us
We miss our resurrection
Then our situations get so bad they stink

In **Going Through a Storm** he told us:
Your storm is your gateway to better opportunities
God will stop your storm when your boat gets full
...So don't fret
We encourage our storms by giving in to them
Sit down and stop acting a fool
...Yo boat ain't even full yet!

In **Why Do We Go to Church** he told us:
We don't go without eating food but we'll skip church
And don't even realize the importance
Of the spiritual meal we've missed
Our commitment is so weak that we'll quit God
For things so dumb it doesn't make any sense to list

In **Scars** he told us:
Jesus put on flesh to feel our pain
He had scars because He survived
Scars don't bleed and are not sensitive to the touch
So we need to stop hemorrhaging
And thank God we're alive!

Thank you Reverend John L. Bowen Sr.
...For all your words of wisdom!

I Don't Know Why
...But I Can Tell You Who

I don't know why little children
Are let down time & time again
But I can tell you who
Will fill-in as that
Mother, father, sister, brother or even a best friend

I don't know why some people
Can't handle life's disappointments
But I can tell you who
Will love you through all your pain
And end your torment

I don't know why this world
Is so wicked, evil & the exact opposite of just
But I can tell you who
Can ease the pain and will never break your trust

I don't know why some people
Drink and smoke their lives away
But I can tell you who
Has healing power to help them see a brighter day

I don't why so many people
Hang on to hurt, pain & despair
But I can tell you who
Will help them find release by showering them with care
I don't know how to explain His love
But I know it exists
When you've tried everything and it fails
Try Jesus and learn how to resist
Then wave good-bye
...As all your fears are dismissed

Which Tool Is in Your hand?

The church exists and is alive today
Because Christ gave our predecessors some rules
Yeah He talked the talk
But He also walked the walked
When He died...He left us the tools

Cement, nails, bricks and mortar
Are the tools He left His sons and daughters
They make for a good, strong, solid foundation
To show the perfect body of Christ to this wicked nation

But somehow things have gone terribly wrong
We've lost our tools as we've traveled along
This Christian journey we walk day to day
Our new motto should be: "Don't do as I do, do as I say"

You see we've picked up some new tools
Tools Christians shouldn't possess
Like bulldozers, chisels and jackhammers
And other destructive tools that cause distress

Did you know satan goes to and fro
Looking and searching for someone to temp?
He's looking for us, the children of the Most High
Those of the world are exempt

It seems in our attempt to stomp on the devil
He's grabbed and taken hold of a foot
And we're allowing him to hold on
And hitch a ride everyday
When we really should've shook

You know like, shake, shake, shake
Shake the devil off?
But he's in our ear saying stupid stuff
Like: "If you walk away, you soft."
And stuff like:
"You remember how good this used to feel."
And, "No one will get hurt if you do it just once."
And we fall for it, forgetting someone's always watching
And their faith could be hurt by our stupid stunts
Upon this rock I build my church
And the gates of hell shall not prevail against it
The devil got some of us fooled so well
He speaks and we jump in an instant
David said: "I foresaw the Lord always before my face
For He is at my right hand that I may not be shaken."
Any Christian who thinks the Lord is not with them
I tell you you're sadly mistaken

Where much is given much is required
And God gave us His very best
So let's reunite and fight the devil as one
There are more blessings when we pass this test
When you feel like the world's against you
And you're in your darkest hour
Knock the devil down and put your foot his neck
Remember Jesus gave us the power
Let's build each other up
Instead of tearing each other down
Because it's not each other we need to defeat
Pick up your bible and hit the devil with the Word
And his tail we will spiritually beat

Cement, nails, bricks, mortar
Bulldozers, chisels and jackhammers
...Which tool is in your hand?

A Faithful Man

Moreover it is required in stewards
That a man be found faithful
(1 Corinthians 4:2)
He is also upright, dedicated, trustworthy and capable
Everything he touches is blessed
And for that he's truly grateful
When his cup runneth over
He helps others to show he is thankful

Who then is a faithful and wise servant
Whom his Lord has made ruler over his household
(Matthew 24:45)
He takes direction from the man upstairs
And this is why he is the mold
He walks in the authority given him
And he doesn't abuse his control
Trusting the Lord, he releases his cares to Him
Then he patiently waits on His mysteries to unfold
He loves and respects his pastor
And he fights to carry out his vision
Using what his pastor instilled in him
When it's time to make every decision
Obedience & determination drives him
So he completes every task with precision
He knows saving the lost and keeping the saved
Is his only mission

The law of his God is in his heart
For none of his steps shall slide (Psalms 37:31)

Jesus Christ is his foundation and his guide
He knows patience is a virtue, so he keeps a steady stride
He never worries about what he doesn't have
Because he knows God will provide
He thanks Jesus for giving him the gifts to lead
To counsel & to teach
He opens his heart & gives love & guidance
To those within his reach
He encourages, uplifts and protects
Confidence he doesn't breach

He is like a tree
planted by the streams of water (Psalms 1:3)
Though he carries a tremendous load
His demands are seldom a bother
He was taught morals, value, courtesy & respect
By his mother & his father
So he protects & provides for his family
And he sets high standards for his sons & daughters
To love, honor and cherish his wife is what he learned
While in the hands of the potter

The steps of a good man are ordered by the LORD
And he delights in his way
(Psalms 37:23)
The world is full of many great Christian men
And we celebrate them today
We hope you feel loved and appreciated
And on the Lord's side we hope you stay
We thank God for you
And that He protects & keeps you, is what we pray

Thank God for faithful men!

A Virtuous Woman

Who can find a virtuous woman?
For her price is far above rubies
She's kind, loving, fair
Devoted & faithful in all her duties
She's not afraid of the snow for her household

For it is clothed in red
Her children are raised with a loving hand
And she keeps them spiritually fed
She pushes them to do their best
And lets them know they can succeed
She also shows them the way by the examples

Of her actions, conduct & deeds
The heart of her husband safely trusts in her
And that trust will always last
She shows him devotion & TLC
And her cares to Jesus she casts
She's a leader who rules with a very firm hand
But is still gentle in all her ways
God is first in every situation
So she'll remain blessed for all her days
She's special because her kind is rare
Women like this are hard to find
Her Bible is her compass so decent & in order
Is how she keeps those around her in line

She says what she means & she means what she says
And it's always said with love
Her words are filled with such love & kindness
They could only come from above
She lovingly embraces anyone who crosses her path
And she does this from the very start

Genuine concern & care for all
Because she's a caretaker from the heart
A dedicated, trustworthy & committed friend
An asset to any team
She keeps a warm smile on her face
And she laughs when she really should scream

Today we celebrate women with well spent years
Who have helped celebrate life as well as shedding tears
Let us rejoice with these extraordinary women of God
A celebrations is what is truly deserved
We've been blessed to know & love them
And this love we must all preserve
For your selfless contributions to womanhood
We owe you this dedication and so much more

Congratulations virtuous women
…Proverbs 31 women to the core!

His Outstretched Arms

His outstretched arms…
Can take the pain away
His sustaining power kept you in the past
And it will continue to keep you today

His outstretched arms…
Can take the needle out of a vein
Give you continuous sunshine
When all you've ever seen was rain

His outstretched arms…
Can turn an abusive hand into a loving embrace
This hand will now caress
When it used to slap your face

His outstretched arms…
Can change your volatile disposition
By holding you close, drying your tears
And giving you the love you've been missin'

His outstretched arms…
Will erase childhood pains from your remembrance
Rearrange your life until you won't recognize yourself
Because there will hardly be a resemblance

His outstretched arms…
Will take you from the beaten path
To a road full of success
Where you will forever feel His comfort
And live highly favored & blessed

His outstretched arms…

What Do You Say?

Some say, "Take the easy route
You know…Fit in."
I say, "Never bend."
This is where it begins
But start here and it will never end
Following your friends and your next of kin
Trend after trend and sin after sin
You're helping the enemy win

Some say, "Life is too short, why second guess?"
I say, "That's why we should try to do our best."
Strive to pass every test
Why settle for less and create a mess?
Of course everyone will be put to rest
But don't you want your soul to be blessed?

Some say, "Why not, we all gotta die some way?"
I say, "What kinda mess is that to say?"
God has a plan and I pray
Every day, every day and every day
That His grace and mercy will allow me to stay
Until He says it's time for me to lay
And that I'll be awakened by the first trumpet
On that great day

Some say, "Does Jesus really love me?"
I say, "So much He died for you on Calvary."

The greatest love of all comes from He
Without Him there would be no Heaven for you & me
The wages of sin is death don't you see?
But not only does He love you, but all three
The most powerful union ever, the Holy Trinity

What do you say?

Sometimes I Can Hear the Lord Say...

Sometimes I can hear the Lord say:
I'm beyond sick and tired of the conformity
This sin sick world ignoring me
Walking around with your chest stuck out
Like I have to allow you to exist
Ask Sodom and Gomorrah
I can deal with situations like this

These days are full of self-fulfilling prophecies
And evil debauchery
A mockery to my Son the Christ
Not many think twice
About what they could
And should be doing with their life
Too many are mentally destructing
Too busy making twerk videos and lusting
I'm the only right in this world and you resist it
You spit me out like I'm poison
Spend earnest time avoiding

Who else tells you to love one another
And to treat each other right
No one because this world tells you
Your purpose is to stay out all night
Drinking, cursing and starting fights

Whatever image dominates a man's mind
Will become his reality
That's why you get into the trouble you do
I have a Will and that will is strong
But you a have pretty strong will too

Allow me to introduce you to your will
Cursing, cheating, back biting, lust, patron
Gucci, fighting, over indulgence, cell phones
Pornography, lying, stealing, hate
Malice, killing, fornication, rape
False testimonies, laziness, gossiping, greed
Lack of faith, fear, conformity, smoking weed
I could go on but I'm sure by now you get the picture
Not many pick up the Bible anymore
Hustler and *Playboy* have replaced reading scripture

You treat my sanctuary like it's your living room
In it you curse, lie, cheat and steal
My name is now just as common as your sin
Not many revere it
And to those of you who don't
Its power will never be real

One day I'm coming back for a remnant
That seemingly gets smaller as the days go by
Too many of you value the opinion of your peers
You think of me often but you're too ashamed to try
Because it's not popular to trust in me
I'm frowned upon in the in crowd
And to the elite I'm taboo
I just have one question

Which one of these social misfits
Has a Heaven or a hell in which to put you?

At Least Change the Picture on Your I.D.

Our lives are open books
And I wish more Christians would
Think about the message our lives give
We should never misrepresent God

Don't shame God
By living a life He wouldn't live

He paid the cost, by dying when we were lost
Something only He could do
So stand when it seems hard
Because He left us the trump card
And the power to make it through

When we decide to wear the label "Christian"
Our old I.D. expires
In order for the Christian I.D. to be effective
We must shed our worldly desires

We are no longer slaves to sin
Because He bought us for a price
He shed His precious blood on Calvary
The least we could do is submit
And allow Him to clean up our sinful lives

Did you change the picture on your I.D.?

Searching

Searching for understanding
Longing for love
On a quest to find knowledge
That can only come from above
I need to feel your presence
And I desperately need it now
The mysteries of life are in your hands
I know you can show me how
Now unto Him
Who can do exceedingly, abundantly
Above all we can ask for
You can take this bitter me and misery
And turn it into so much more
So now I'm prostrate before your throne Lord
And I appeal to you today
I humbly seek your healing
Please cleanse me in every way
Break me, mold me & make me
Into a vessel you can use
Save me from my own wisdom
And with you, I know I won't lose
Edify me, teach me, purge me
Heal me of my infirmities
Release me from bondage & shame
Help me hallow thy name
Searching for understanding
Longing for love
On a quest to find knowledge
That can only come from above

Called to Responsible Living

Called to responsible living
Is very fitting for this event
It's time to take a close look at our positions
And re-evaluate our purpose for being sent
Christians should be like bodybuilders
Helping to strengthen the body of Christ
Responsible living in word and deed
Is the strength that helps keep saved lives

Sometimes the only way some people know us
Is by the report other people give
What does your report say about you?
Is everything they say about you true?
Does every negative thing they say
Line up with what you actually do?
Weight your harvest

Have you ever stopped to seriously think
About how you affect the lives of others?
How many bad seeds have you sown
In comparison to the good seeds?
How many times have you passed up a gossip session
To meet someone's needs?

How much more good could you give
To this troubled, dying world
By encouraging some single mother
Or some young troubled girl

If you tell her she's beautiful
From the moment you walk into her life
I promise you can sit back
And watch her bloom into a flower
If you show her how to respect herself
And how to carry herself as a woman
That abusive man in her future won't have any power

If you stopped inflicting pain
And instead you piled on joy
By stepping in to replace an absentee father
In the life of a wayward boy
If you lavished him with love
And showed him he has a purpose in this life
If you showed him a man
So he could see the possibility of what he could become
You could give him an outcome
Opposite of being a father on the run

We don't sit on the front row during worship service
Because we're special and we deserve it
We sit on this row to let the congregation know
We are ready and willing servants
We don't turn up our noses when people come near
In fear that they'll take our seat
If they need our seat we'll gladly stand
Because it's their needs we're here to meet
We don't wear white on the 1st Sunday
Because we're holier than thou
It simply symbolizes holy & uniform servants
Willing to serve right now
We don't have to figure it out on our own
...Jesus already showed us how

We should take new members under our wing
When they join church
And visit members in the hospital
When we hear they've been hurt
We should show love and concern
And help them carry their heavy load
And be there when they fall off the beaten path
To pick them up, dust them off
And show them the right road

We should tell them what God loves
Even when that's not what they want to hear
Be there for them no matter what
And then they'll keep us near

We have been *called* to responsible living

Why Lord Why?

Why Lord Why...Why do you love me like you do?
You introduced yourself to me while I was in the womb
Told me in this world I'd face difficulty
And advised me not to let the bitterness consume
But I forgot and let my emotions get the best of me
You told me, you were all I needed
And not to get caught up searching for love from men
Told me not to think too much of myself or get conceded
And both I've done time and time again
Why Lord, Why...Why do you love me like you do?

I go against you repeatedly
I'm unworthy of your agape love
But still you give it freely
It's not like you don't know the wrong I do
You're with me every day
Holding and comforting me
Desperately trying to lead my way
You constantly guide me out of my mess
The mess I inflict upon myself
The mess I somehow manage to find again
In my quest to find temporary happiness & financial wealth
Why Lord, why...Why do you love me like you do?

You're just like the wind
I can't see you with my physical eyes
But I can feel you on & underneath my skin
I was so soaked in sin only you could wring me in
You took my sin soaked body & squeezed me until I was dry
In spite of me, you saved me from the penalty of sin
So my soul will never have to die
Why Lord, why...Why do you love me like you do?

Touch His Garment

We are imperfect women
Crying out to a perfect God
Screaming out in desperation Lord please help me!
I am diseased!
I misbehave because I am depraved
I have not fully surrendered
Therefore I remain enslaved
This cry comes from the pit of our souls
We earnestly beg the Lord to take control

Picture this:
A woman is lying on the ground in the desert
Her throat dry like cotton because she's water deprived
Lack of food has made her body extremely weak
She's beyond exhausted, barely alive and she can't speak
Every time she claws at the ground
In an attempt to move forward
The sand consistently slips through her fingers
She is overcome with fear and defeat lingers
She remains in the same diseased place
In the same diseased state
Her disease killing her at a very slow pace
She thinks to herself
If I could but touch...

Just like this woman
This world hasn't been nice to us
It's let us down time and time again
From mama & daddy to so called friends
And last but not least ladies...These men

Our hearts have been ripped out
Thrown on the ground
And repeatedly drug through the mud
Now they have grown cold and hard
And we have lost all hope
Of ever seeing the happiness that once was

Anger, sickness, sadness...An abundance of frustration
Cowardice, confusion, temptation
Too much time spent trying to shake desolation
Misplacing the core of us...Now we only see red
Just a few of the side effects
Of being let down, mistreated and misled
So we gossip, fornicate, attack each other
Commit adultery and covet
We are bitter, jealous, prideful, hateful, spiteful
And we act as though we love it

We worry and torture ourselves
With the most trivial things
And we suffer from the torment and heartache it brings
What is going to happen to my relationship?
Will some other woman steal his heart?
Or will he betray me by using her body parts?
Will my children turn out right?
Will my fellow sister in Christ start a fight?
How will I make it since my job let me go?
Can I trick them into believing I'm not human
If my emotions don't show?
How did I ever get into this situation?
How can I figure this out on my own
How can I avoid future devastation?
How can I get over on someone else
To get enough money to pay my bills?
How can I play surgeon and operate on myself
So my heart can heal?

Will this man treat me like the last?
How can I get this video in my head
To stop replaying my past?
As complicated as these things may sound
I promise a simple task will end this confusion
Reaching out from your dark place
And touching His garment is the solution

Remember that lady lying on the ground in the desert?
Ladies, that's us
Although we all inhabit a variety of desert places
And no two are the same
Trust me ladies, He can help us all
There is power in His name
And there is enough power in His garment
To rid the world of everything that ails it
Seeking Him and touching His garment
Would definitely be to our benefit

Today I offer you a healer
His power is unlike anything you have ever known
Anything you could ever imagine
And anything you have ever been shown
If you already have Him
That's definitely a plus
But having Jesus and holding on to our issues
Puts the spotlight on our lack of trust
We don't have to remain stuck in captivity
The key to getting out of our desert place
Is to tap into His power
Today is the day and now is the hour
Ladies I beg you

...Touch His garment

My Soul Has Been Anchored

No longer do I blow helplessly in the wind to & fro
I am enslaved by the Master and proud to say so
He attached an anchor to my soul that keeps me immovable
Though my life is a raging sea
I'm being pushed and pulled from side to side
But these trials can't move me...*My soul has been anchored*

Controversy surrounds me daily
Sorrow haunts my dreams
Despair should have me in bondage...Or so it seems
Depression should have its way in my life
Complacency's roadblock should've stopped my success
But I'm anchored by the best...*My soul has been anchored*

I should be...Dead and sleeping in my grave
I should have slit my wrists
I should be out of control not knowing how to behave
I should be hooked on drugs & alcohol
I should be ready to give up on everything
Just throw in the towel and walk away from it all
But I can't...*My soul has been anchored*

I come from neglect, abuse, incest and pain
But God put something in me that continuously sustains
It won't let me to give up on life and breathing
He put something in me
That makes me want to leave a mark in this world
Worth leaving...*My soul has been anchored*

Let the storms rage, let it rain, let it pour
Let the winds blow, though they are fierce and cold
I'll sway but I won't be moved
The Lord attached an anchor to my soul
*My soul has been anchored...**In the Lord***

He Broke Me

He is the potter and I am His clay
God is molding me into a vessel
And He breaks me every day
I am His investment
Not because of how good I am right now
But because of the masterpiece He's molding me into
Every time He breaks me, I'm better off
And I've overcome a few more things I used to do

He doesn't trust me with me and for that I give thanks
He gently places and centers me on His wheel
Smooths my rough parts
And places fresh clay in my blanks
With strong, firm hands He molds, sculpts & shapes

Although being broken is uncomfortable
And at times I think I want Him to stop breaking me
I am thankful He breaks me again & again repeatedly
I know in the end, a much better person I'll be

When I cursed her out and tried to fight
He broke me because I wasn't right
He is patient and He takes His time to get me just right
He spit in the dirt, placed the mud on my eyes
And restored my sight

When I was constantly lying down confused
...Getting up misused
When my sexual prowess got the best of me
And I continuously did things I shouldn't do
He broke me
Like when I slept with him out of wedlock
And when I slept with him when he had a wife
He broke me and put me on a path to a better life
I lay on the floor broken into pieces
But He didn't leave me there
He got rid of my pride and unwillingness to care
In my brokenness, He gave benediction to my pain
He took away the fear & confusion
So I could maintain
He has an uncanny way of quenching my desire
He took away the lusts of my flesh
So I could soar higher

He broke me down on my Damascus road
Got rid of wicked things that held a tight hold
And took me from Chestnut Street to Straight Street
He chose me and He chooses what He will make me
Though my sins have greatly diminished
He knows while I'm in this body, I'll never be finished
So He breaks me again & again
Because I don't fit His mold
But when He is done and I'm out of this body
...I will come forth as pure gold

For Once in My Life

For once in my life my smile is sincere

   For once in my life I live without fear

For once in my life my happiness is true

   For once in my life I recognize my value

For once in my life my joy is authentic

   For once in my life my thoughts aren't demented

For once in my life my disposition is calm and sweet

   For once in my life I truly like the people I meet

For once in my life I'm proud of my actions

   For once in my life I determine my own satisfaction

For once in my life I walk with my head held high

   For once in my life I'm not afraid to try

For once in my life my emotions don't take over

   For once in my life my heart is not growing colder

For once in my life I have control

   For once in my life I have a savior for my soul

The Construction & Rebirth of Danielle

Take me as I am
For broken I've already been
God has already prepared me
I'm done adjusting for men

He chipped away my anger, bitterness He stripped away
He gave me humility, patience & a love that's here to stay
Now my daily prayer to Him, is that He will lead the way

He told me not to rush around
In search of my one true love
Instead I should spend that time with Him
Patiently waiting for instruction from above

All my life I've moved on my own
The result was mistake after mistake
I gave freely of myself to all the wrong men
That's why it all ended in heartache

So I surrender to you, Lord
It's your guidance I seek
I promise not to move on my own again
I'm waiting for you to speak

Thank you Lord for showing me the error of my actions
I know you've given me the man
Who meets your satisfaction
As I awake to the dawn of a brand new day
The horizon is a sight to see
My rebirth has occurred
And now I am content
…Content with just me

A Brand New Outlook

I no longer look at the world through the eyes
...Of the abused
Of someone sick and tired of being used
To fulfill the sick selfish needs of men
I now choose something worthy...My view I extend

I no longer look at the world through the eyes
...Of confusion and doubt
No more settling for less and taking the easy route
I'm challenging myself to the core
I now look at the world through the eyes
Of a woman who wants more

I no longer look at the world through the eyes
...Of defeat
I no longer feel less adequate
Than the successful people I meet
I've encouraged myself to move forward with my head high
And it will remain in that position until the day I die

I no longer look at the world through the eyes
...Of self-pity
Take ten steps back and miss me with that sympathy
Never again will I cry for the past
I have arrived at Victory Road at last

I no longer look at the world through the eyes
...Of anger
I no longer lash out because I know the danger
It's counterproductive...A complete and total waste
I'm really loving this new outlook
...Can't you see it on my face?

The Dawn of Danielle

Unbeknownst to my past, a new dawn awaits
It takes courage to shake the chains away once they break
And I've got that and more
I'm very excited because I know I'm about to soar
To heights mine eyes have never seen
To places I've only heard about
Through other people's dreams
It seems this new dawn has awakened the beast
The least I could do is feed it and unleash
I need it because without it
My dawn will have risen in vain
This beast will help me carry out my mission
Of changing the game
Of burying the old one along with my pain
My brain doesn't compute failure & it's not in my vocab
This new dawn is the introduction to my future
I must admit it seems pretty fab
I've conquered the demons of my past
I'm walking into a new existence with pride
Never again will I run away...Never again will I hide
So move to the side
And oh yeah...Please don't kill my vibe
I've waited a long time for this & some say I deserve it
When He plucked me out of the darkness of last night
God told me I'm worth it
He said you gave Hell one heck of a fight
A new dawn I give you, a better day to live through
Do you boo!...And that's just what I intend to do
I'm free from my past, no more living in hell
You have just witnessed
...The dawn of Danielle

Blank Page

On February 11, 2013,
I turned the journal of my life to a new page
The page is blank, it's new, it's fresh
What will I write? ...What will I do? ...Where will I go?
There is a great expanse of nothingness
As far as my eyes can see
Fear creeps in
So I call on my Lord and Savior Jesus Christ
I seek His wisdom and guidance
When I doubt or ask questions
He speaks to me as quick as a flash
I don't like the past I'm leaving behind
It's all I know, it's comfortable
(The future I have for you will bring you great joy)
How will I pay my rent?
(Don't worry about rent; move from this place)
Where will we go?
(A temporary place is already provided)
How will I feed my children?
(I feed you and your children every day)
What if I lose my job?
(The cattle of a thousand hills are mine)
What if my children rebel?
(Lead a child in the way...You've done that, right?)
What if I can't make it on my own?
(Lo, I am with you always; you are never alone; I'll
remain right by your side)

I trust you Lord
(I know you do & you will reap the benefits
of your trust & faith, I love you child)
I love you too, Lord
I close my eyes
With great trepidation,
I place my feet on fresh new pavement
Not entirely sure of where I'm being led
Pavement full of so many opportunities
So many possibilities
I regain my composure
I stand up as straight as a board
I hold my head high and take a deep breath
He promised to get me through this
Not that it would be easy
The possibility of difficulty
Doesn't sway me in the least
...I trust Him
For the first time in many years
My smile is genuine
This new smile covers my face
I begin to walk
One strong step at a time
...Into my destiny!
Thank you, Lord!

SNEEK PEAK INTO MY NEXT BOOK

little girl lost...Grown Woman Found
Volume 2: What I've Learned

The poetry I selected to share from the next book is
from the section entitled:
The State of Black America
...This is a personal cry to my people.

"The broken pieces after the storm are meant for us to
hold on to survive, not to live on...Let go!"
—Reverend John L. Bowen Sr.

The ABC'S of Wrongful Conviction

Assiduously, atrocious alignment of abominable acts
Blatant, brutal blemishes of brazen banishment
Cowardly cunning, calculated, crooked convictions
Diabolical, devilish, detestable deeds & dereliction of duty
Excessive exclusion, egregious eradication & ethnic entombment
Fermented felonious falsehoods and fictitious fantasies
Grandiose, gaudy, glorification of gruesome grievance
Hushed, heinous, haunting humiliation housed in hate
Ignorantly inflicting injustice & infractions to infringe innocence
Jealously jeering justice & jack legged justification
Knowingly keeping the keys of kindness and knowledge
Legalized lawlessness, lynching, liable leaches & lowdown lies
Monstrous, misconduct, misdeeds and mocking malfeasance
Negation, Nullification and neglect of natural need
Obliterating, offensive, ongoing outcries of oppression
Perpetual, parasites pointedly positioning paralysis
Quick quiet quests to quell questions
Republic, repulsive repugnant, refusal of rights
Strategic, sneaky scandalous sabotage
Tormenting the truth through torturously twisted transgressions
Unfathomable undercover usurping & ugliness upheld
Villains vicariously and viciously violating victims
Wanton wickedness ways
Xclusion
Yearning to yank the yoke
Zoneless zeros

How I Came Here: The Story of a Slave Girl

One day we was in ah hut
Mama was cookin' an sangin' us a song
Papa was fixin' on duh table
When dese mean white men came along

Dey buss in duh doe
An papa got upset
Mama grab me an Sissy
An tole us not tuh fret
Papa tried tuh stop em'
But dey buss his head open wit a gun
So mama drag us out duh doe
An tole us both tuh run

We didn't get to fah
An foe long dey had us on dis boat
A whole lot uh us wuz goin' sumwhere
But wheh we was goin' nobody know'd

It was so miny uh us we could hardly move
Mose of em' got so sick dey died
We din't know where Papa an Sissy wuz
Mah mama prayed a lot but mosely she jus cried

Afta a long time on duh boat
We come tuh sum peculeuh land
Dis white man say he ah massuh nah
An tole all who wuz alive tuh stand

He say, I needs tuh makes my profit
An to miny uh y'alls is dead
I needs fuh y'all tuh look like sumthin'
So go get clean up in dat shed

Massuh sold me tuh dis white man
Cuz he say he wuz duh highest bidda
He sold mama tuh dis'n udda white man
An say I cain't go wit huh

My mama grab an hold on tuh me
I know she din't wanna let go
But dat white man hit huh wit dis big stick
An knock huh tuh duh flo
He told huh, you iz my heffa nah
An yo youngin is'n his
Now get yo black butt on backa dat wagon
Foe you get sum moe uh dis

Mama look up at me
Wit big tears in huh eyes
An wit blood on huh fingas
She point up t'woeds duh skies

Den she say, baby juss pray
So dat's juss what I do
Duh lass thang I heard mah mama say
Is don't worry chile, God is wit'chu

She been gone uh long time nah
Sometimes I's tired
But I do as I's tole
Cuz I memba mama always said
Girl yo strenff comes from duh Lord

Which *They* Are You?

They came over with
Big boats and big chains
For us to...
Pick they cotton and grow they grain
They whipped our fathers
And manhandled our mothers
They raped our sisters and killed our brothers
They took our religion& heritage
And broke our foundation
And on our sweat and our blood
They built this nation

Oh but...

They gave up their lives to segregate schools
All they wanted was equality in the rules
They were beat brutally and never did see
The freedoms we now abuse so easily
They fought with every ounce of strength God gave
They had no idea their seeds
Wouldn't know how to behave

Cause now, you see...

They hang out on street corners and claim sets
But they blame the white man
For the trouble they get
They ain't interested in working
And won't help raise they kids
They never give a second thought
To what the civil rights activists did
They used to fight but now they shoot each other
Do we need to wonder why
There's a shortage of black brothers?

Now...

They hang out in the clubs
And drink all night
Instead of staying home with they kids
And raising them right
They think it's cute
To be smacked up by they man
And when he gets locked up
They visit him all they can
They sell they body &
And use drugs in the home
This is the reason
Good family values and morals are gone

But thank God!!!

They bring they kids up in church
They teach em' about
Self-value, determination & worth
They teach em' about
The man who set us all free
And tell em'
He paid the price so there is no fee
They show they kids mother and father roles
And the others could too

Black people I ask you today

...Which **THEY** are you?

Legacy

What is the legacy you'll leave?

Slangin', bangin' and sangin

About sex drugs and rock & roll?
Or some thick cutie slidin' down a pole?
Black people, where's the control?
We gotta get a hold of this generation
And help save their souls

What legacy will follow your name?

How you stole a wallet and stuck it up your sleeve?
How you so hard, when the popo came, you ain't leave?
You was a stone-cold killer
That was too scared to succeed?
Had a free pass to Heaven…But didn't believe?

Is your legacy worth anything?

Black people, it's time to rethink our ways
Turn over a new leaf and see some better days
Put down the alcohol and the purple haze
Stop thinking about us and ours only
And help collect the strays
Just because you not drinkin' and druggin'
Don't mean that kid mama not
And he can't deal with it so he turns to the rock
On the corner slangin' good crack,
Until the cops blow up his spot
Now the judge is tellin' him
20 years is what you got
That is, if he don't get shot

Or strung out...Or beat to death
Callin' out to a mama who ain't there
With his very last breath
You just might be the only chance he got left
But you missed a chance to help because you slept
Minding your own business
You turned a blind eye & his help you kept

Black people, what is the legacy you're leaving?

It's time to stand up and proclaim your emancipation
Get out of your comfort zone and help this generation
That's facin' destruction and devastation
Young scholars, doctors and lawyers wastin
Their God-given talents and givin' up on education

Do you even know what a legacy is?

A legacy is defined as anything
Handed down from the past
And if we don't hand down something better
Our people won't last
Because our legacy is a name brand bag
We rob Peter to pay Paul for a brand new Jag
Ain't paid our rent
But braggin' about poppin' a tag?

What is your legacy?

Keepin' up with the Joneses is what it's all about
Walkin' around stuntin' and frontin' like you got clout
Man this makes me wanna shout, pull my hair out
Cause all they got is frustration and doubt

They ain't stable and don't have enough confidence
To know they're able
So put your money where your mouth is
Or better yet on the table
Teach them about them God, not the Blac Label
I feel like I'm trapped in a nightmare
Or some kind of fable

Take control of you legacy!

It's time out for passing the buck
We need to come correct
Because this generation right here
Is feeling the effect
Instead of achieving dreams he's the #1 suspect
I can't believe these are the types of things we respect
We choose & select to disrespect and neglect
The legacy our forefathers left us
They were beat in riots and didn't even cuss
Had to walk miles to work and still didn't take the bus
And guess what?
They left that legacy for us!
But we've let them down and betrayed their trust
We meant something to them
But what do ours mean to us?

So since a legacy is left by those who've gone on before
Remember your bad decisions will open a door
For some kid to walk through searching for more
Stitch your legacy tight and watch them soar

The Legacy!

The Unheard Cries of Our Children

Poverty is a silent killer...
It seeps into our brains and causes a chain reaction
A distraction from reality...Such a tragedy
It grabs our sons and daughters
And prepares them for slaughter
By their throats
It throws them into chaos and confusion
Teaches them how to misuse their intelligence
With an illusion

Scare tactics and fear are instilled
It holds them violently against their wills
As victims of poverty, these kids ain't got nothing
But that nothing means a lot
Running up to take that nothing...Will get you shot
They feel thrown away and misused
By everyone they meet
But deep down attention is what they seek

Their attitude is:
If negative attention is the only attention I get
Then I'mma make sure we spend some time
From the principal's office
To police stations and the courts
One way or another...I'mma get mine
If negative attention is the only attention I get
Then I'mma live life to the fullest
I'mma get bad grades cuss, skip school
Have unprotected sex
I'mma even see if I can dodge this bullet

Our children are crying out in pain
But gunshots ring louder and covers their cries
Mothers & fathers can't come to their rescue
Because a wool has been pulled over our eyes

Our children are crying out in frustration
But defeat is covering the sound
They desperately need a way out
But it seems there's no one around

Our children are crying out in agony
And their cries are going out in vain
Another body just hit the ground
He's taken away, the pavement is blood stained

Our children are crying out in anger
They'll do anything to get our attention
Deep inside of the misdeeds and attitudes
You'd hear a heartbeat if you'd just listen

Our children are crying out in fear
They're tired and don't want to go on
But they'll do what they have to do to be heard
Because by no means are they weak
…But they are strong

Another shot just banged
And it now echoes in the distance
The lives of three young black males
Just changed in an instant
As the smoke clears and crowds disburse
The scene before their eyes couldn't be worse
Two young men lie face down in a puddle of blood
Because another young man ignorantly held a grudge

Beautiful black child
When I look into your eyes
I should see strength, courage and determination
But self-hate, violence and anger are all I see

And I'm sick and tired
Of the cries of our children going unanswered
Of violence ripping through the hood like cancer
We must transfer these negative feelings
Of self-hate and worthlessness
Into something with a more positive aspect
And not only listen to the cries of our own children
But take a moment to help another child get on track
The fact that one child crying is enough to spoil many
Is not something I have to tell you
I compel you to search your heart
Do something about the dilemma
Remember the first step is always the hardest part

It's time for black America
To re-write the lives of black youth
Take the sting away from poverty
By teaching our children the truth
Everyone reading these words has heard a child cry
...What did you do about it?

The Unheard Cries of Our Children!

I Wondered...

When I stepped in to the room
I saw two girls sitting on one chair
With long faces and blank stares
Not even a hint of life was there
One slid down the chair and crashed to the floor
In some weird delayed reaction
The other one finally looked toward the door
She still had the needle in her arm
Drifting off to some faraway land
Where she couldn't feel pain
Where the sun shined all day
And there was never any rain

I wondered what caused this defeat
And why they didn't have enough strength to sustain?

To my right, a man slouched on a mattress
His body nothing more than a shell
His eyes deeply embedded in hollow sockets
They were completely empty
There was no story to tell
His image was similar to that of a ghost
He was covered from head to foot in soars
His veins were all collapsed
But he desperately searched for more
He had to get that one last high
...Even if it would truly be his last

I wondered why he allowed his life to be haunted
By whatever happened in his past

His spitting image sat crouched in the corner
He couldn't be any older than age nine
The tracks of crocodile tears were evident on his ashy face
By two thick wet, moisturized lines
His skinny arms were wrapped tightly around his thin legs
Which were folded closely to his chest
On his frail shoulders he carried the weight of the world
He clearly didn't have an ounce of strength left
This boy that should be out running and enjoying life
Was sitting in this house surrounded by defeat and death

I wondered why he had to endure this hurt
And if he could muster up enough strength
To take another breath

Then suddenly Jesus appeared next to the boy
He touched him on his shoulder
He gave him the strength he desperately needed
Not to give in to this lifestyle when he gets older
He whispered in his ear, his purpose in life
Told him to enjoy the rest of his childhood
Explained to him in detail how to get over this hurdle
And assured him he could
Though his eyes had cried a river for all he'd seen
It's said, the eyes that's washed with tears see the best
Because he was able to recognize God
In the midst of his pain
Now he can put his mind at rest
Jesus touched him, healed him and restored his joy

I no longer have to wonder…About this little boy

Liberty & Justice for All...

Land of the free Home of the brave
I wouldn't trade it for anything
Even though I'm still enslaved

Victim of a system that wasn't designed to benefit me
You have enough gall to say I should be content
Because I'm better off than where I used to be?
You love to remind me
There's a black family in the White House
Then you self-righteously ask me
How much more do I want
I ask how much more do you have?
How much of a payoff will it take
To stop this 400 + year haunt

To be perfectly honest
I don't want you to give me anything
Just open that door you shut and I'll get it myself
Because it often seems my intelligence and drive
Isn't enough to get around your roadblock to wealth

Until then don't tell me I should stop complaining
About America's foot on my neck
About racial profiling, wrongful convictions
And a total lack of respect
Neglect, handouts, ghettos and slums
The system smiling in my face as if we're chums
About homelessness, helplessness
And an abysmal state of distress
Recidivism, low retention
And kids not expected to pass the next test

America has grown by leaps and bounds
As far a Black America is concerned
But the fact that we have not yet arrived
Is a hard lesson we continue to learn
We must continue to leap hurdles
If justice and equality we hope to find
It won't be an easy feat but a hard mountain to climb

Land of the free Home of the brave
I wouldn't trade it for anything
Even though I'm still enslaved

But where is my piece of pie?
What happened to my 40 acres and a mule?
And all the other things that were voiced
But never carried through
Instead held over my head like a tool
40 acres and a mule has set us up to fail
All we ended up with is a limited amount of food stamps
And 20 years in jail
They tell us these lies and we're naïve enough to believe
So we limit ourselves
And teach our children how NOT to succeed
I'm patiently waiting for the scales of justice to balance
Searching for success remains a challenge

Where is my piece of pie?
You constantly spoon feed me Small quantities of equality
Pacify me with welfare, WIC, government housing
And other forms of your suppressing diet
Keeping me at bay in hopes I'll keep quiet
These things are designed to keep us disillusioned
Don't try to deny it

Where is my piece of pie?

Our vision is tunneled
Like horses running the Kentucky derby
We hold on to scraps
And losing these scraps is our biggest worry
We need to stop being complacent
With handouts and pats on the head
And stop settling for what they give us
Educate our people and work jobs instead

Welfare lines, subsidized housing and GA
Hinder and obstruct our emancipation in every way
They send the illusion they're building us up
But they're actually keeping us bound
America will only give us so much
And that little bit is designed to hold us down

Where is my piece of pie?

Land of the free Home of the brave
I wouldn't trade it for anything
Even though I'm still enslaved

America...
        The Great American Melting Pot...
            Land of the free...
                Home of the brave...
                    Liberty and justice for all...

On the surface America appears to be Heaven-sent
But scratch the surface...And you can read the fine print!

(Offer only available in some areas... Subject to approval... Prices may vary and are subject to
change...Void where prohibited)

ACKNOWLEDGEMENTS

little girl lost...Grown Woman Found is finally done and there are many, many people who can be held responsible for its birth. First and foremost none of this would be possible without the gift of words **God** placed inside of me and His continued guidance, instruction, and direction. God has opened so many doors for me in spite of me. Thank you **Jesus** for your love, mercy and favor!

My husband, **Shawn**, you are a very special man who will always hold a special place in my heart. I thank God for you and I thank you for all you have been to me and the kids. It takes a strong man to stand in the gap and raise four children he didn't father all while still trying to figure out life for yourself. I applaud you...You did a great job! You have made a tremendous impact in our lives and I thank you from the bottom of my heart! You are a testament to how hard a man will try when he is given the opportunity! I also thank you for the love and support over the years. You have been our rock, covering, provider, protector, and the man of God we needed to help see us through. For more than a decade we have shared love, laughter, anger, frustrations and just about every other sentiment known to man. Each one was a building block necessary for our journey together and we are stronger because we had you to share these moments with. I look forward to the decades to come!

To my children, **Lamont, Latrez, BriAija and Destiny**, thank you for helping me see every cloud has a silver lining no matter how dark it gets. Each of you have added value to my life in your own special way. You have given me hope and determination to make something out of the nothing life I had before you. **Lamont**, you taught me how to laugh and perfected my ability to fuss. In every situation you were always there telling a joke to lighten the mood or doing something extremely goofy; causing me to fuss you out! Your personality, outlook on life, and intelligence will take you far in this life! I love you, son!

Latrez you taught me the power of relying on self and determination. From a small child you were always comfortable being alone and didn't need an entourage or the acceptance of others. You have a drive that's hard to find in today's youth. Once you put your mind to something...It's a wrap! Those two characteristics among many others will help you soar in this life! I love you, son!

BriAija, you came along as I was finally figuring out what being a mom is all about and taught me to how to be courageous because change is okay. You are a very beautiful, self-reliant, intelligent young lady who is fun, energetic, caring and compassionate. You remind me of myself in many ways...Especially that mouth! LBVVS! At an early age, you have somehow found a balance between fun and responsibility. I pray to you keep it! With all the many talents you possess, I have no doubt you're going straight to the top! I love you, daughter! **Destiny**, where would we all be if you hadn't come to join our family? Though you have always been blood, your moving to Minnesota with us has opened us all up to new ideologies, viewpoints, challenges and successes. You taught me the true meaning of persistence. In addition, you taught me that any relationship worth having is worth fighting for. I am glad God gave me the blessing of being the one who fought for you...You are truly worth it! You are the prize...Don't sell yourself short! Someone once said: An overpriced item is often overlooked by those who can't afford it...Or deserve it! (Let that marinate!) I love you, daughter! I would not be the woman I am today if God hadn't blessed me with the four of you and I thank Him daily! As you embark upon your own individual journeys of life, always remember to keep God first! Also, never forget the foundation we laid for you and the tools we have equipped you with. Remember the things you were taught and things you have witnessed in our home both good and bad and use them as stepping stones to propel you into the bright futures you deserve! I love you all with a mother's relentless and never-ending love! The sky is your limit; shoot for that and nothing less!!

Mama, mama, mama, thank you for giving me life and for setting me up on a foundation of self-worth and value. No matter how hard times got, you made sure I knew I was beautiful and intelligent; I never have and never will forget it. Every time I hear *Amazing Grace,* I think of you. I know in my heart you did the best you could and I love you for that! You rock my friend! (Insider) I love you with all my heart!

Granny/Allean Sr., I am your namesake and although I have toiled with my name in the past, I couldn't be more proud today to be the one to bear your name. You are a resilient woman with a strong disposition and ruthless endurance and I love you for all you are. I don't know where the Ward family would be today if it had not been for the persistence, determination, and downright stubbornness you instilled in us. I love you!!

My adoptive parents, **Pastor John L. Bowen Sr. & First Lady Bettye Bowen**, thank you for welcoming me into your family and loving me unconditionally. **Dad** I thank you for teaching me God loves me and that He will help me pick up the pieces of my brokenness! I also thank you for the countless counseling sessions & teaching moments that helped mold me into the Christian woman I am today. Finally, I thank you for taking me in and loving me as if I were biologically yours. I couldn't love you more...Wink!

Mom, I thank you for accepting me and the relationship. It has been said countless times that a great woman stands behind every great man and I thank you for being the one who stands behind my dad! Thank you for the love, encouragement and for brutally putting me in my place when I need it! I will always remember, "This ain't no night club!" LBVVS!

To the best in-laws in the world! **Eric & Denise (Pa & Ma Tetter)**, I love you both with all my heart! Thank you for accepting me and the kids and loving us as if we were your very own! We have shared so many fun times with you and your love & encouragement is out of this world! I look forward to the years to come!

To my siblings, **Tangula, Adonis, Maurice and Kurtis,** thanks for putting up with me when I was mean and surly. Our childhoods were not picture-perfect but when we didn't have anything at all...We always had each other. In spite of it all, we laughed way harder than we cried. Looking back now, I wouldn't have wanted to share our many memories (good, bad & horrible) with any other group than you four goof balls!! I love you all and I pray God will give each one of you peace. Let go of the past and live life...You owe it to yourselves!

To my aunts and uncles: **Pamela, Robert, Henry, Cornell Jr., Dennis, Karon, Alean, Shawn & Marisa**, I love you all and I thank you for stepping in with all of us when the time came. You all wore many hats in this family and was always willing to take off your "assigned hat" and pick up the one that was needed at the time! Aunties became moms, counselors and referees; uncles became dads, friends, bodyguards, and voices of reason. I couldn't have asked for a better bunch of cool & crazy people to call my very own! I have to give special recognition to my **Auntie Elzora** who passed away before I had a chance to know her. I have heard the stories and I know in my heart she would've fit right in with the madness! I love you, Auntie!! I would be remiss if I didn't share my gratitude to a special uncle and aunt. **Uncle Dezuan**, you were not born to Cornell & Allean Ward, but I wouldn't have known it from your actions. As far back as I can remember, you were there, loving and nurturing us. More than that, I can recall the countless times you interceded and protected us when we needed it most. I love you with all my heart and I thank you from the depths of my soul! **Auntie Von**, I thank you for being a great woman of God. In many ways I believe the Lord has been able to use me to a greater extent because I modeled my Christian walk after yours. You are a woman who loves the Lord with your whole being and it shows in everything you say and everything you do. Of all the women I have met in life, you are hands down the most humble, loving, and supportive and I'm honored to call you my auntie! Last but not least, I thank you for inviting me to your church GMV! That invitation changed my life!

To **my cousins,** I love all 500 of y'all!! LOL! I am so proud of us! We are all breaking milestones and setting in motion better futures for the Ward Clan! Not only are we graduating from high school, but we are getting college degrees! No more generations of welfare...We work jobs and have careers! To God be the glory!!

Special thanks to my three special cousins, **Tysha, Mandi and Tomi,** for always being there for me! Not only when I was up the street and around the corner but even now that I'm hundreds of miles away, you are proof that love knows no distance. I cannot recall a challenging time in which one of you or all of you haven't been there for me. From those encouraging late-night conversations, to fights (with other people and each other), there is no doubt in my mind that I wouldn't be the woman I am today if it wasn't for you beautiful ladies! **Tysha** wind-milling me with those hard feet and showing me how to really torture someone; **Mandi** right next me screaming and witnessing Ms. Mary and hiding me under groceries so I could spend the night; **Tomi** Evel Knieveling me off that bike and getting me in trouble for doing your homework are all very traumatic experiences but so worth it and hilariously funny now that we can look back at them! I love you all dearly and I am so proud of the ladies you have become. To the best friend I have ever had in my life, **Bridgette,** where do I begin? Thank you for showing me what a sister is. Thank you for your consistent encouragement and support. Thank you for always having a plan and for having a selfless heart of gold. You taught me many, many things but at the top of the list is the true meaning of "Friends don't let friends drive drunk." Although neither of us drinks, we somehow found a way to apply this encouraging phrase to just about every facet of our lives. I like to think we are better women because of this very direct, very brutal honesty. Many women could benefit from this type of love for one another. I feel honored to call you my best friend and no one could ever come close to understanding the appreciation, gratitude, and love I have for you.

To my sister **Jill**, and very first editor for *little girl lost*!! Thank you for your input, direction and correction on this book. I also thank you for your love and support over the years. It has truly meant a lot to me and my family!!

To my sister, **TeeTee Gwen**, you are a wonderful woman who voluntarily stepped in when needed and became a second mother to my children. My gratitude to you cannot be summed up by words. From the bottom of my heart I thank you for the countless times you have taken my children home and loved them as though they were your very own. I could never pay you for what you do but please know I appreciate you and I am blessed to have you in my life. I pray one day to have a heart as big as yours!

I have been blessed with a large group of women as a support group. I have to shout out my sisters: **Linda** *(Proverbs 31 Woman to the core)*, **Edith** *(Songbird Extraordinaire)*, **Phat** *(Hairdresser to the stars)*, **Vanessa** *(10 lbs of love in a 5 lb bottle)*, **Sandy** *(Hey Beautiful...I'm right here)*, **Tanya** *(Will start a fight for me in a dark room)* **Michelle** *(The best co-chair EVER)*, **Audua** *(Late love is REAL love too!)* & **DeDra** *(My friend until the end...Our time has come!)*. *I thank you all* for loving on me, encouraging me, and for having my back. Each of you have added an indescribable amount of confidence, resiliency and fun to my life! I love you ladies!!

To my "Speaking out loud" **Marlea**, I never knew we would grow so close the day I walked into that cube! Thank you for allowing me to bounce countless ideas off you. Thank you for helping me combine my many ideas for the book cover and for all your excitement and encouragement.

To my Sister Authors, **Dr. Sheronda Oridge, Tinithia "Da Black Pearll" Warren and Kahladee,** thank you all so much for embracing me and my writing, unselfishly sharing your wisdom and experience, including me in your events, and investing your time to keep me encouraged through this process. We definitely need more women of color who lift each other up instead of tearing each other down. Again I thank you, my loves! For those of you reading these words...These are three very intelligent, powerful writers...Purchase their books! You will NOT be disappointed!

The book's cover is the first thing a potential consumer will see; therefore accolades must be given to **Regina Wamba** of MaeIdesign. Thank you for somehow getting into my brain and creating the cover I saw but ironically couldn't quite put into words. I'm honored to have my name scrawled across the beautiful work of art you created.

Once a book has been opened, the first thing the reader will notice is the layout and appearance of the words. And boy oh boy was this formatting a struggle!!! Arrrgghh!!! There were many irons in the fire on this one including myself. I labored relentlessly going back and forth sitting in front of computers for hours and hours and hours trying to get this thing formatted! Thank you Jesus that's over!! Shout out to everyone who tried their best to help me birth what I had envisioned! Thank you, **Amy Eye** of The Eyes For Editing and **Tinitha Warren** of Words of Wise Dome...It's FINALLY done! Thank you so much for your time and effort!

To **my church family at Greater Mount Vernon M.B.C.,** from the bottom of my heart, I thank each and every one of you for encouraging me and supporting my writing. You helped me realize my poetry was a gift that needed to be shared! Although there are too many to name, many of you gave me the encouragement needed to step out on faith with my poetry. Others stayed on my case year after year, fussing at me to finish this book and letting me know you had my back. I am grateful to be a part of a wonderful, loving and supporting body of Christ. I love you all!

Finally, I would like to say thank you to **everyone** who loved, encouraged, and even those who tolerated me when I was doing too much. I thank everyone who played a role in my life, no matter how big or small, whether it was to build me up or tear me down. I thank you with all my heart. Whatever your role was, you helped a little girl lost become the WOMAN I am today! God Bless you all!!!

Ps 34, 77, 109, 120
1 Sam 13:20
John 10:10
Mark 5:34

Made in the USA
Charleston, SC
04 October 2014